D0484715

Perfect Phrases for Business Proposals and Business Plans

Also available from McGraw-Hill

Perfect Phrases for Performance Reviews by Douglas Max and Robert Bacal

Perfect Phrases for Performance Goals by Douglas Max and Robert Bacal

Perfect Solutions for Difficult Employee Situations by Sid Kemp

Perfect Phrases for Customer Service by Robert Bacal

Perfect Phrases for the Sales Call by William Brooks

Perfect Phrases for Executive Presentations by Alan Perlman

Perfect Phrases for Business Proposals and Business Plans

Hundreds of Ready-to-Use Phrases for Winning New Clients, Launching New Products, and Getting the Funding You Need

Don Debelak

McGraw-Hill

New York Chicago San Francisco Lisbon
London Madrid Mexico City Milan New Delhi
San Juan Seoul Singapore Sydney Toronto

The *McGraw·Hill* Companies

Copyright © 2006 by The McGraw-Hill Companies, Inc. Printed in the United States of America. Except as permitted under the United States Copyright Act of 1976, no part of this publication may be reproduced or distributed in any form or by any means, or stored in a data base or retrieval system, without the prior written permission of the publisher.

5 6 7 8 9 0 FGR/FGR 0 9 8

ISBN 0-07-145994-4

This is a *CWL Publishing Enterprises Book* produced for McGraw-Hill by CWL Publishing Enterprises, Inc., Madison, Wisconsin, www.cwlpub.com.

This publication is designed to provide accurate and authoritative information in regard to the subject matter covered. It is sold with the understanding that neither the author nor the publisher is engaged in rendering legal, accounting, or other professional services. If legal advice or other expert assistance is required, the services of a competent professional person should be sought.

—*From a Declaration of Principles jointly adopted by a Committee of the American Bar Association and a Committee of Publishers*

McGraw-Hill books are available at special quantity discounts to use as premiums and sales promotions, or for use in corporate training programs. For more information, please write to the Director of Special Sales, Professional Publishing, McGraw-Hill, Two Penn Plaza, New York, NY 10121-2298. Or contact your local bookstore.

 This book is printed on recycled, acid-free paper containing a minimum of 50% recycled, de-inked fiber.

Contents

Contents

Contents

Contents

Contents

Contents

Preface

We live in a sound bite world today, in politics, in news, and increasingly in business. Sixty-page business plans are initially screened in five to 10 minutes and business proposals sell or don't sell in even less time. Bankers and investors scan plans and quickly capture their essence in three to four sentences:

ABC's space [the current popular term for market niche] is GPS (Global Positioning System) for truck fleets that allow fleets to provide their customers accurate tracking information. ABC sells equipment to fleets at cost, collecting per delivery tracking fees. ABC's edge is better tracking information than a Federal Express type system and an automatic e-mail system that advises customers of projected delivery dates. The extra cost to the trucker is $1.50 per delivery while ABC's per-delivery tracking costs are $0.75.

Writers of business proposals and business plans have two challenges:

- generate enough interest so their documents survive the initial screening process and

■ convince people to accept and move forward on the actions requested by the proposal or plan.

This book will help readers create "power paragraphs" in their proposals and plans with high-impact phrases that can help them with both challenges. The power paragraphs are designed to quickly communicate a company's essential benefits in order to move past the initial screening process. The paragraphs and phrases are also designed to help pass the final evaluation of the target customer, investor, or other principal. Adding perfect phrases in each section of the document frames the section to the writer's purpose and steers the reader to understand and accept the writer's points.

The book is separated into two parts: business proposals and business plans. Part One covers perfect phrases for business proposals. It is formatted to follow a typical scorecard, whether formal or informal, that clients or potential partners use when evaluating a plan. Part Two on business plans follows the same format as the business proposal section with each chapter covering a key item on the potential investor's or bank's scorecard. Each chapter deals with one of the items on the scorecard, offering phrases that position the business as a "can't miss" opportunity.

Finally, a formatting note: Chapters 1 and 10 have black edges. This has been done purposely because these two chapters serve as the foundation for the perfect phrases sections on business plans and business presentations that follow. We added the black edges to make it easier for you to quickly refer to these chapters

This book is not meant to be a complete guide to writing a business proposal or plan. It is meant to add value to those documents by providing power paragraphs and phrases that quickly communicate points that will generate a positive response from readers. If you are writing a business proposal or plan for the first time you might also refer to a book that covers the basic points. Here are some of my favorites:

Business Plan Kit for Dummies by Steven J. Peterson and Peter E. Jaret (Hungry Minds, Inc., 2001). Includes a CD-ROM.

The Successful Business Plan: Secrets and Strategies by Rhonda Abrams and Eugene Kleiner, Fourth Edition (The Planning Shop, 2003).

Successful Business Models: Surefire Ways to Build a Profitable Business by Don Debelak (Entrepreneur Press, 2003).

Persuasive Business Proposals: Writing to Win More Customers, Clients, and Contracts by Tom Sant, Second Edition (Amacon, 2003).

Writing Winning Business Proposals: Your Guide to Landing the Client, Making the Sale, and Persuading the Boss by Richard C. Freed, Shervin Freed, and Joe Romano, Second Edition (McGraw-Hill, 2003).

Acknowledgments

To John Woods of CWL Publishing Enterprises who asked me to write this book and to Bob Magnan and Nancy Woods, also of CWL for their help in editing the manuscript and for keeping me focused on the target of straightforward effective communication. And thanks to Donya Dickerson of McGraw-Hill who initiated this project.

About the Author

Don Debelak, president of DSD Marketing, has spent his career marketing products for new and small businesses, writing numerous business plans for raising money, both from investors and banks. Don has worked with all types of businesses, with many contacts as a consultant for the University of St. Thomas Small Business Center (St. Paul, Minnesota), from a small one-person service business to high-tech ventures that raise money to launch a new product. He has been the monthly columnist of "Bright Ideas" for *Entrepreneur* magazine since 1999 and is the author of nine books, including *Successful Business Models: Surefire Ways to Build a Profitable Business* (Entrepreneur Media, 2003), *Infiltration Marketing: Achieving Astounding Sales Increases on a Very Low Budget by Entering Your Customers World* (Adams Media, 2000), and *Streetwise Marketing Plan* (Adams Media 2000). Visit his Web site at **www.dondebelak.com**.

Perfect Phrases for Business Proposals and Business Plans

Part One

Perfect Phrases for Business Proposals

The Business Proposal Scorecard

P eople who receive business proposals have widely vary-
ing agendas, and they actually review and score proposals based on their particular circumstances and needs.
This is different from business plans where readers have a more
or less standard scorecard for judging the viability of the plan.

For business proposals the client will evaluate proposals dif-
ferently, and it is difficult to accurately predict how the client will
score your proposal. But I've still found it helpful to have your own
scorecard to make sure that you've included all the key points
that sell proposals. As in the case of business plans, a successful
proposal depends on having the right phrase for all the key
points to sway the client over. Often clients will only remember
three to four phrases from a proposal, so you want those phrases
to present you and your proposal in the best possible light.

Business Proposal Scorecard

1. **Client Needs:** Address Perceived Needs (Chapter 12)
2. **Project Goals:** Perfectly Match the Client's Goals (Chapter
   13)

3. **Expertise:** Target the Client's Exact Needs (Chapter 14)
4. **Targeted Message:** Adjust to Client Circumstances (Chapter 15)
5. **Deliverables:** Fit the Client's Goals (Chapter 16)
6. **Cost:** Deliver High Value (Chapter 17)
7. **Value Added:** Clear Benefits for the Customer (Chapter 18)

Chapter 1
Typical Format:
Matching Expectations

Business proposals can cover a wide variety of topics, but these are the five most common types of proposals:

1. Outside project proposal—a project done with little company involvement, such as a research study of marketing and partnership strategies in the juvenile products market.
2. Integrated project proposal—a project done in close cooperation with the client's employees, such as implementing a Six Sigma quality control system in two of the client's remote factories.
3. Ongoing service proposal—a proposition to form a continuing relationship, in contrast with doing a project, such as signing on with a PR firm for two years of PR services.
4. Joint cooperation proposal—two or more companies cooperating in a way that provides benefits for both or all. For example, three dental companies with complementary

product lines could cooperate in marketing and sales activities to cut expenses and provide more extensive sales coverage.

5. Partnership proposal—two parties working in a formalized agreement to achieve an objective. For example, a wireless hardware and a software company might form a partnership to develop a product that can handle 20 wireless units connected to one high-speed Internet line.

Part two of the book will follow a format similar to the format of the business plan section, with each chapter covering a key item on the business proposal scorecard and then offering an example of a perfect phrase for each of the five types of proposals.

Proposals are typically offered in either a letter or formal format. The choice of the format you use is typically client-related. Some clients prefer letter proposals, some prefer formal proposals, and others prefer a letter proposal first and then, if they like the letter proposal, a formal proposal. Typically the best approach is to ask the client which type of proposal he or she prefers.

The letter and formal proposal formats outlined below are similar to most business proposals offered today, but they are not rigid. You can adjust them in order to present your case more clearly. Your proposals should be fairly short, though; if you make them too long, people will skim them and miss some of your more important points. The perfect phrases in the following chapters are meant to be key points that lead into each section of the proposal so that readers who skim the document will clearly understand your proposal's benefits. As in the business plan section of the book, each of the following chapters of perfect phrases will identify the part of the proposal in which the perfect phrases belong.

Letter Proposal Format

Letter proposals can be from one to five pages long, but I've found the best length is two to three pages. That is long enough so that the client knows you've considered your proposal carefully, but not so long that the client feels you are trying too hard to get his or her business.

1. **Brief Description.** State in one sentence the purpose of the proposal. For example, "This is a proposal to develop a waterproof barrier for SpaCovers, hot tub, and spa foam core covers."

2. **Current Situation.** Explain the client's or prospective partner's situation that your proposal is responding to. In the case of a joint cooperation or partnership proposal, explain your situation as well. This section provides information about the current situation and why the current situation is creating problems, needs, or opportunities. (Point 1 on the scorecard)

3. **Goals.** State here the goals of the client or partners as they relate to the problem or opportunity. The goals should relate to what the client or partner has told you, as well as corresponding to the results you can actually achieve. For example, a hospital's problems might be that it takes too long to record patient information and that too often information is inaccurate. The hospital's goal might be to reduce the time spent recording a patient's information from 15 to 10 minutes and to have 95% of the reports error-free. If you can meet those goals, you state them in the proposal. If those goals are ambitious, you would state that the goals are to cut the time to input patient information and to

increase the accuracy of the reports. (Point 2 on the score-card)

4. **Approach.** In this section, give a broad description of what you are going to do and then reinforce that the approach will be successful, by offering success stories if possible or by explaining your company's expertise. For example, "Knoblach Associates will implement the Six Sigma program with a combination of classroom training, mentoring, and monthly review meetings. This is a similar approach to the one successfully used at KGB Manufac-turing and Air Flow Filters, both of which had a fully oper-ational Six Sigma program within nine months." (Points 3 and 4 on the scorecard)

5. **Action Plan.** List specific actions you will take for the client. The action plan is often an attachment if the list of action items is too long. (Point 5 on the scorecard)

6. **Deliverables.** If the proposal or project includes any deliv-erables, specify what they are: for example, five- to 10-page monthly reports, completed design packages, or number of print and TV ads. (Point 6 on the scorecard)

7. **Costs.** For client proposals, list what the client is expected to pay. For joint cooperation or partnership proposals, list who will pay what portion of the costs. (Point 7 on the scorecard)

8. **Conclusion.** In this section, focus on explaining the cost-benefit ratio of the proposal, basically stating that the client or partner receives benefits that more than justify the cost. (Point 8 on the scorecard)

Formal Proposal Format

Big companies often prefer formal proposals. The information in a formal proposal is similar to the information provided in a letter proposal, but it is more detailed and complete. Formal proposals also typically are in binders and use graphs, pie charts, and lots of visual aids. An excellent reference book for preparing professionally looking proposals is *Handbook for Writing Proposals* by Robert J. Hamper and L. Sue Baugh (NTC Business Books, 1995).

1. **Executive Summary.**
   a. *Brief Description.*
   b. *Situation Analysis: State the client's needs.*
   c. *Client's or Partner's Goals.*
   d. *Approach: In broad terms, describe the way you will approach the problem.*
   e. *Key Factors for Success: Tell why your firm is ideally suited to provide the service.*
   f. *Pricing and Cost-Benefit Analysis.*

2. **Scope of the Work.** This section defines your role in a project. For client-based proposals, this section explains the hierarchy of the program. Your company might be totally in charge of your part of the project, delivering a final result, you might be working under the supervision of a client employee as part of a team, or you might be working with another vendor. For partnerships, you want to define the scope of the partnership, which includes the partnership's goals, the roles and responsibilities of each partner, and how the partners will interact.

3. **Initial Analysis.** You want clients to understand that you considered many options before selecting the one you

feel will work best. I've also found that clients might prefer an option you considered but dropped. If you include those options here, the client will often come back and ask for a proposal for the option he or she prefers. (Points 1 and 4 on the scorecard)

    a. *Approaches Considered.*

    b. *Positives and Negatives for Each Approach.*

    c. *Approach Selected,* with a brief explanation of the benefits or the approach.

    d. *Examples of Success* for the approach you've selected.

4. Key Targets.

    a. *Performance Goals.* List the overall goals, of which there could be two or three, plus targets within those goals. For example, if a hospital's goal is more accurate reports, then you should list three to four specific ways in which the hospital would like the reports to be more accurate. (Point 2 on the scorecard)

    b. *Other Goals.* This could include items the client has specified in your initial discussion, such as utilizing input from regional managers, ensuring that 20% of the members of the quality control staff are Six Sigma black belts, or coordinating ad campaigns with major trade shows attended.

    b. *Positives and Negatives for Each Approach.*

    c. *Approach Selected,* with a brief explanation of the benefits or the approach.

    d. *Examples of Success* for the approach you've selected.

5. Key Components. List the major items or actions that you will provide based on the proposal to the client. In the case of a joint cooperation or partnership proposal, list major actions that both parties will provide.

6. **Areas of Special Expertise.** Explain the specialized and, preferably, unique expertise that your company has in any of the key components. This section should show why you are the ideal supplier. (Point 3 on the scorecard)

7. **Pricing or** (for a joint cooperation or partnership proposal) **Resources Committed.**

8. **Cost-Benefit Analysis.** Demonstrate why the benefits outweigh the costs.

9. **Implementation.**

   a. *Client-Provider Interaction.* Provide an overview of how the companies will work together, such as weekly or monthly meeting or reports or periodic phone conversations. (Point 5 on the scorecard)

   b. *Action Timetable.*

   c. *Deliverables.* (Point 6 on the scorecard)

   d. *Resources Provided.* Specify for both parties such things as access to customer lists, engineering drawings, utilization of office space, or other resources.

   e. *Responsibilities.* Specify for both parties. This is an especially key section if you are proposing a joint cooperation or partnership agreement.

10. **Project Team Members.** Provide a paragraph on each member and include full résumés in the attachments.

11. **Pricing.** (Point 7 on the scorecard)

12. **Warranties or Guarantees** (if offered).

13. **Cost/Benefit Analysis.** (Point 8 on the scorecard)

14. **List of Past Projects and References.**

Chapter 2
Client Needs:
Address Perceived Needs

'
've found that successful business proposal writers have discovered that people approve or take actions for their own reasons and not for the proposal writer's reasons. So your plan needs to focus on what the client feels are its needs and not on what you feel are the client's needs. A winning proposal states that you understand the client's needs, that you have grappled with ideas for meeting those needs, and that you have come up with an action plan that will address those needs. For joint cooperation and partnership proposals, you should also state your company's needs.

Power Paragraph

As in the business plan section, each chapter in the business proposal section deals with one key issue on the evaluation scorecard. You will find it easier to first write your power paragraphs with perfect phrases before writing the proposal. That will help you focus on the elements that will sell your proposal. You can then place the power paragraphs into the right sections of your proposal. In the letter proposal, you may be able to use each power paragraph of perfect phrases only once.

The rest of the chapter offers you the perfect phrases for power paragraphs for each of the five types of proposals using examples from various businesses. I've used businesses from the business plan section, as you are already familiar with those companies' goals. Each set of businesses will be used in two chapters as examples. Choose the example closest to your own proposal as a model for your perfect phrases and power paragraphs.

Elements of the Power Paragraph

- **First goal:** State what the client feels are its needs.
- **Second goal:** State the immediate purpose of meeting those needs.
- **Conclusion:** State the longer-term benefit of meeting those needs.

Sample Power Paragraph

This power paragraph is for Innovative Tooling, a tooling distributor that provides custom specialty tools for 125 custom machine shops in Texas and Oklahoma. The company is proposing to take over the tool design for RJB Manufacturing in return for a monthly retainer (an ongoing service proposal).

RJB Manufacturing is considering dropping its custom manufacturing sales efforts because custom jobs require too much engineering support. *[First goal: state what the client feels are its needs.]* The personnel required for custom jobs creates excess overhead, which is choking profits on the entire product line. *[Second goal: state the immediate purpose of meeting those needs.]* If RJB can reduce the overhead related to custom jobs, it will be able to keep promoting custom business, which currently represents 18% of RJB's business. *[Conclusion: state the longer-term benefit of meeting those needs.]*

Applicable Proposal Sections

Letter Proposal

    2. Current Situation

Formal Proposal

    1b. Executive Summary—Situation Analysis

    3. Initial Analysis

First Goal: State What the Client Feels Are Its Needs

I feel the number-one mistake people make in proposals is to list what they feel are the client's needs, rather than focusing on what the client feels are its needs. When listing needs, quote the client directly, if at all possible. If you are doing a joint cooperation or partnership proposal, also be sure that you state your needs as well as the client's needs, with equal emphasis.

OUTSIDE PROJECT PROPOSALS

Peterson's Residential Solution (offers residential service for mentally challenged people living in family, apartment, or group settings). *Proposal for locating funding to provide services for the Johannsen family's 19-year-old son.*

The Johannsen family wants to find funding for job training and enrichment activities for their son that allow him to continue to live at home.

INTEGRATED PROJECT PROPOSALS

Outsource Computing Power (runs high-end enterprise resource planning [ERP], customer service, and accounting software for its customers). *Proposal to work with Premier Manufacturing's IT department to develop a cost-benefit analysis for a project that will integrate ERP software into its manufacturing operation.*

Premier has three large clients that are requesting it to upgrade its ERP software. Premier IT staff is looking for assistance in choosing and implementing an ERP software solution.

ONGOING SERVICE PROPOSALS

Tickets-on-Line.com (a Web site where people can buy and sell unwanted purchased tickets). *Proposal to handle returned and unwanted tickets for the Indiana Dome for 2006 and 2007.*

The Indiana Dome's policy is to offer ticket refunds or exchanges up to 72 hours before an event. The cost of handling these returns and the resulting loss of revenue cost the Indiana Dome over $450,000 per year. Slow handling of refunds is also a major source of customer irritation. The Indiana Dome is looking for a better way to respond to requests for ticket refunds and exchanges.

JOINT COOPERATION PROPOSAL

Builder Bob (manufacturer of play tables for children two to seven that targets the over 20,000 child-care centers in the eastern United States that serve over 30 under-five-year-old children per day). *Proposal for joint sales activities with Creative Playthings, which manufacturers creative play toys, with an emphasis on toys that can be used to build structures.*

Creative Playthings and Builder Bob have built strong regional reputations, Creative Playthings in the Southeast and Builder Bob in the Midwest. Both companies want to broaden their sales penetration to additional markets, but individually lack the sales and marketing resources to build a new market.

PARTNERSHIP PROPOSAL

All Kitchen Distributors (rack jobber distributor that purchases space in supermarkets, convenience stores, and large drugstores). *Proposal for a partnership with Pampered Chef to supply a new brand to dedicated kitchen stores and kitchen departments in upscale stores.*

Pampered Chef wants to expand by offering a new brand of upscale kitchen products that are sold to retailers rather than through home parties, in order to generate higher profit margins. All Kitchen Distributors also wants to expand its market to include higher-margin dedicated kitchen stores and high-end department stores.

Second Goal: State the Immediate Purpose of Meeting Those Needs

Many proposals fall by the wayside because the client decides not to address its needs. Reaffirming the importance of meeting those needs helps encourage clients to move forward with the proposal.

OUTSIDE PROJECT PROPOSALS

Peterson's Residential Solution. The son needs job training and enrichment activities to fulfill his full potential, and living at home in a loving family atmosphere provides the son emotional support as he adjusts to the working world.

INTEGRATED PROJECT PROPOSALS

Outsource Computing Power. Upgrading to a new ERP software system, rather than simply trying to improve the current software, will meet Premier's key customer demands and it will cut Premier's overall inventory costs and shorten Premier's manufacturing cycle.

ONGOING SERVICE PROPOSAL

Tickets-on-Line.com. Recovering just half of the refund money would improve the Indiana Dome's operating margin by 5% and outsourcing the refund process would save $45,000 in operating costs.

JOINT COOPERATION PROPOSAL

Builder Bob. Expansion to a major new market, with a sales force already established in that market, could potentially increase both companies' sales 25% to 75%.

PARTNERSHIP PROPOSAL

All Kitchen Distributors. Both Pampered Chef and All Kitchen Distributors are facing increasing competition in their traditional markets, and they need to diversify to continue their sales growth and to maintain their existing margins.

Conclusion: State the Longer-Term Benefit of Meeting Those Needs

Your statement about why meeting the need is important should typically be specific to the situation. The benefit as presented in the conclusion should be broader, with a strong impact on the potential client.

OUTSIDE PROJECT PROPOSALS
Peterson's Residential Solution. Finding funding that allows the son to stay at home provides him the best opportunity to thrive as he makes the transition from school to the working world.

INTEGRATED PROJECT PROPOSALS
Outsource Computing Power. An upgraded, state-of-the-art ERP system will position Premier as a viable growing vendor with a full electronic data exchange to support even the largest of Premier's potential customers.

ONGOING SERVICE PROPOSALS
Tickets-on-Line.com. Outsourcing the ticket refund and resale process will cut costs, increase profits, and provide better customer service, enhancing the Indiana Dome's reputation as a leading nationwide entertainment venue.

JOINT COOPERATION PROPOSALS
Builder Bob. A cooperation agreement will allow both Creative Playthings and Builder Bob to be considered as major suppliers to the day-care market and to set the stage for sales to major day-care chains east of the Mississippi.

PARTNERSHIP PROPOSALS

All Kitchen Distributors. Expanding into the new market will allow both companies to significantly participate in the high-margin cooking school/kitchen store market that is sweeping the country.

Chapter 3
Project Goals: Perfectly Match the Client's Goals

You start an effective proposal by communicating first that you understand the customer's needs. The next step is to show your proposal matches the client's goals. Clients are typically drawn toward proposals that offer perfect synergy with their needs and goals and that synergy offers you a strong chance of obtaining their business.

Power Paragraph

Elements of the Power Paragraph
- **First goal:** State what the client feels are its goals.
- **Second goal:** State why that goal was chosen.
- **Conclusion:** State that the goal is achievable.

Sample Power Paragraph
This power paragraph is for Innovative Tooling, a tooling distributor that provides custom specialty tools for 125 custom machine shops in Texas and Oklahoma. The company is proposing to take over the tool design for RJB Manufacturing in return for a monthly retainer (an ongoing service proposal).

RJB Manufacturing's goal is to cut its overhead for custom jobs by 65%. *[First goal: state what the client feels are its goals.]* A lower overhead will be more affordable during periods when there are no custom jobs to work on. *[Second goal: state why that goal was chosen.]* RJB can achieve this goal by outsourcing tooling design and procurement on an as-needed basis and by eliminating the separate custom job-quoting department. *[Conclusion: state that the goal is achievable.]*

Applicable Proposal Sections

Letter Proposal
   3. Goals

Formal Proposal
   1c. Executive Summary—Client's or Partner's Goals
   4a. Key Targets—Performance Goals

First Goal: State What the Client Feels Are Its Goals

I find it helpful when writing a proposal to think that the client's job is to clear out its in basket or to-do list. The client has projects or problems that need to be addressed; an effective proposal helps clients see that they are wiping a project off the list. Your proposal will sell when you do the best job of eliminating a to-do action on the client's list.

OUTSIDE PROJECT PROPOSALS
Peterson's Residential Solution (offers residential service for mentally challenged people living in family, apartment, or group settings). *Proposal for locating funding to provide services for a family's 19-year-old son.*

The family's goal is to have the son live at home while still receiving financial aid for the services he needs.

INTEGRATED PROJECT PROPOSALS
Outsource Computing Power (runs high-end enterprise resource planning [ERP], customer service, and accounting software for its customers). *Proposal to work with Premier Manufacturing's IT department to develop a cost-benefit analysis for integrating ERP software into its manufacturing operation.*

Premier wants to both upgrade its ERP software and train its current staff to run the operation. Premier's board of directors has requested a cost-benefit analysis for the program and Premier's IT staff wants to work with Outsource Computing Power to prepare that analysis.

ONGOING SERVICE PROPOSALS
Tickets-on-Line.com (Web site where people can buy and sell unwanted purchased tickets). *Proposal to handle returned and unwanted tickets for the Indiana Dome for 2006 and 2007.*

The Indiana Dome's main goal is to outsource the ticket refund process to cut staff and management aggravation. Problems with refunds consume 40% of the time of ticket office personnel.

JOINT COOPERATION PROPOSALS
Builder Bob (manufacturer of play tables for children two to seven that targets the over 20,000 child-care centers in the eastern United States that serve more than 30 under-five-year-old children per day). *Proposal for joint sales activities with Creative Playthings, which manufacturers creative play toys, with an emphasis on toys that can be used to build structures.*

Both Builder Bob and Creative Playthings have a goal of increasing sales 25% through sales in expanded sales areas.

PARTNERSHIP PROPOSAL
All Kitchen Distributors (rack jobber distributor that purchases space in supermarkets, convenience stores, and large drugstores). *Proposal to partner with Pampered Chef to supply a new brand to dedicated kitchen stores and kitchen departments in upscale stores.*

Pampered Chef, a product manufacturer, and All Kitchen Distributors, a kitchenware distributor, both want to participate in the rapidly expanding cooking school/kitchen store market and the high-end department store kitchen goods market, which is currently dominated by European manufacturers.

Second Goal: State Why That Goal Was Chosen

In this power paragraph, you are trying to reinforce that the client is proceeding on a wise course of action. Stating that the goal chosen by the client makes sense and helps the client be decisive in moving ahead with your proposal.

OUTSIDE PROJECT PROPOSALS
Peterson's Residential Solution. The family feels strongly that for their son to receive services while staying at home would be best for his and the family's emotional well-being.

INTEGRATED PROJECT PROPOSALS
Outsource Computing Power. The cost-benefit analysis is important because the company is considering several other investment options that would leave Premier's IT department with outdated and, in some cases, obsolete software.

ONGOING SERVICE PROPOSALS
Tickets-on-Line.com. The Indiana Dome needs to reduce ticket staff because it is fully utilized only when events occur, which is about 60% of the year. The larger staff expense is an overhead expense the Indiana Dome wants to reduce.

JOINT COOPERATION PROPOSAL
Builder Bob. Builder Bob and Creative Playthings both have excess plant capacity and underutilized equipment. The overhead costs of that excess capacity is sapping both companies' profits. A 25% increase in sales would boost both companies' before-tax profits to 10% of sales.

PARTNERSHIP PROPOSAL

All Kitchen Distributors. Both companies want to enter these markets with an upscale product line because they are high-margin and fast-growing markets that neither company participates in currently.

Conclusion: State That the Goal Is Achievable

You may not be able to meet the client's goal entirely, but you should still assure the client that your proposal, together with other action on the client's part, will meet the goal. If the goal can't be met, the chances are the client will not move ahead with anyone's proposal.

OUTSIDE PROJECT PROPOSALS

Peterson's Residential Solution. Peterson's has been able in the past to combine several funding programs to help families stay together and, while the funding from those programs has ended, Peterson's is confident it can find other funding sources that will allow the son to stay at home.

INTEGRATED PROJECT PROPOSALS

Outsource Computing Power. Outsource Computing Power has done a quick analysis of several implementation options and all show benefits that are at least four times the cost of implementing the program.

ONGOING SERVICE PROPOSALS

Tickets-on-Line.com. Tickets-on-Line resells tickets that people aren't using at over 125 venues across the country and will be able to easily handle the spikes in activity that occur during Indiana Dome events. Tickets-on-Line has 35 customer service personnel on staff who can handle any problems that might occur.

JOINT COOPERATION PROPOSALS

Builder Bob. Both Builder Bob and Creative Playthings sales forces have established relationships in their own regions, with a solid customer base. Having both sales forces add the other company's products should be able to increase both company's sales with only minor increases in sales costs.

PARTNERSHIP PROPOSALS

All Kitchen Distributors. Pampered Chef is an innovative product developer without any experience in retail distribution. All Kitchen Distributors has a nationwide network of distribution centers and sales and service representatives capable of providing the in-depth customer service required by the upscale market. Together the two companies should be able to generate immediate share in the targeted lucrative market.

Chapter 4
Expertise: Target the Client's Exact Needs

Effective proposals target customers' goals and expectations. Once prospects know that you are aiming at the right target, they need to determine if you can do the job. You want to show that your expertise closely matches what the client is looking for. This is usually done in two ways: first by demonstrating experience in the field, typically through a relevant job history, and second by mentioning similar projects you have done with successful results. The most effective way to address expertise, especially in letter proposals, is to state in a power paragraph that you have the experience and then attach a list of work experience and prior contracts that are pertinent to the project in your proposal.

Power Paragraph

Elements of the Power Paragraph

- **First goal:** Explain what type of expertise is required for the project.
- **Second goal:** State your company's special expertise that matches the project needs.

■ **Conclusion:** Summarize your company's relevant experience.

Sample Power Paragraph

This power paragraph is for Esthetics Plus (full-service supplier of skin care products). Esthetics Plus's market niche is spas and salons in California and Arizona that employ professional estheticians. This is a six-month proposal to help start up and run the skin therapy department for Renewal Spas and Salons in Northern California. The proposal envisions training professional estheticians and a department manager so that they can take over and run the program independently. This is an integrated project proposal.

This project requires a person with management experience in the professional esthetician area at one of the elite five spas and salons in the world. *[First goal: explain what type of expertise is required for the project.]* Joan Anderson, president of Esthetics Plus, has extensive experience as both an employee of and a consultant to the esthetician departments of all of the elite five spas and has introduced two new advanced facial treatments that have been adopted by leading spas in New York and Los Angeles. *[Second goal: state your company's special expertise that matches the project needs.]* The company's two founders were employees at Waldorf Luxury Spas in New York and were involved in two upgrades of the professional esthetician department, upgrades that are still being used. Esthetics Plus has participated in planning for professional esthetician departments at 16 spas, including the Hollywood Spa in Los Angeles. See attachment for a complete list. *[Conclusion: summarize your company's relevant experience.]*

Applicable Proposal Sections

Letter Proposal

4. Approach

Attachments

Formal Proposal

1d. **Executive Summary**—Approach

2. **Scope of the Work**

6. **Areas of Special Expertise**

First Goal: Explain What Type of Expertise Is Required for the Project

OUTSIDE PROJECT PROPOSALS

PokerMania.com (site with poker instruction, supplies, accessories, and news on upcoming tournaments by state). *Proposal for the soon-to-open Washington County Race Track card room to offer an interactive computer poker course, with a simulated game environment, to enable new players to learn how to play the five types of card games offered by the card room.*

A poker course requires insight into reading other players, anticipating the odds, and knowing how and when to bluff. A poker course must be taught by an experienced poker player, but most importantly with poker players who have successfully set up poker training sites in the past and understand the needs of novice poker players.

INTEGRATED PROJECT PROPOSALS

MediaTile Smart Signs (signs with wireless connectivity for retail stores, enabling stores to change in-store signs from the office). *Proposal to work together with Supermarket IT Consulting to introduce MediaTile Smart Signs' system in 38 Bob's Produce grocery stores in the Colorado, Wyoming, and Montana markets.*

Supermarket IT Consulting has extensive knowledge of existing supermarket software systems. To introduce a wireless sign system, Supermarket IT needs a company with an in-depth understanding of the wireless sign systems available.

ONGOING SERVICE PROPOSALS
City Course Catering (exclusive rights to staging events, primarily weddings and rehearsal dinners, in two 1920s-era golf course clubhouses). *Proposal to Taylor Kellogg Corporation for hosting monthly anniversary and award lunches and for catering banquets for all employees in July and December.*

Taylor Kellogg's special thank-you luncheons and banquets require a supplier that can deliver events with memorable ambience and meals that are far above a typical catered event.

JOINT COOPERATION PROPOSALS
Johnson Dental (three dentists and two hygienists serving new housing developments). *Proposal to be presented to Briarwood Veterinarians, Curves exercise club for women, KinderCare Learning Center, and Spectacles Opticians shop.*

This project requires a promotional piece that people will save for when they actually need one of the cooperating companies' services. The project should be done by a company that can show at least 10 to 15 samples of highly effective promotional pieces.

PARTNERSHIP PROPOSALS
Gannet Sales (supplies and services complete line of soft serve frozen yogurt and smoothie equipment). *Proposal to French Mountain Bakeries for starting up and running smoothie and soft yogurt stations in 18 French Mountain stores.*

A smooth-running smoothie/soft yogurt product line requires expertise in running a restaurant, the ability to prepare appealing dessert treats other than soft yogurt, and the ability to provide and finance the equipment and smoothie and soft yogurt supplies that will produce an 80% gross margin.

Second Goal: State Your Company's Special Expertise That Matches the Project Needs

OUTSIDE PROJECT PROPOSALS

PokerMania.com. PokerMania's staff of four poker buffs, who are also software engineers, are currently on their fourth generation of computer poker training courses. PokerMania opened about 12 months before the latest Texas Hold 'Em craze and had three years to develop its current level of sophisticated software.

INTEGRATED PROJECT PROPOSALS

MediaTile Smart Signs. MediaTile Smart Signs' personnel include a former supermarket manager and two wireless hardware/software engineers. The engineers developed the supermarket sign system and they would supervise closely the technical personnel involved in this proposal.

ONGOING SERVICE PROPOSALS

City Course Catering. City Course Catering has the ambience in its historic settings, the experience of hosting over 250 events per year, and contract arrangements with two of the region's top restaurant chefs for premier events.

JOINT COOPERATION PROPOSALS

Johnson Dental. Johnson Dental has preliminarily located two direct mail firms that have over five years of experience in preparing specialized direct mail and promotional pieces and that have an in-house creative team.

PARTNERSHIP PROPOSALS

Gannet Sales. French Mountain offers the required restaurant expertise, desirable locations, and restaurants with welcoming layouts that encourage late afternoon and evening visits from teenagers and young adults. Gannet Sales can provide and finance the equipment, maintain the equipment, and provide low-cost supplies to generate the margins required for extended hours at the French Mountain locations.

Conclusion: Summarize Your Company's Relevant Experience

OUTSIDE PROJECT PROPOSALS
PokerMania.com. PokerMania has had over 25,000 people utilize its interactive Web course and has set up training computers at two card rooms in Arizona casinos. No company in the U.S. has more experience setting up interactive poker training courses.

INTEGRATED PROJECT PROPOSALS
MediaTile Smart Signs. MediaTile engineers worked on wireless systems in college and have installed the MediaTile Smart System in 22 supermarkets on the East Coast. The company also uses as a consultant Frank Borton, an engineer who has successfully designed wireless systems for sewage treatment systems.

ONGOING SERVICE PROPOSALS
City Course Catering. Joann Wheelock has owned City Course Catering for two years and has hosted 40 large-scale events, including six special corporate banquets. Prior to owning City Course Catering, Joann was a restaurant manager at two exclusive restaurants for 12 years. See attachment for a complete list of major events.

JOINT COOPERATION PROPOSALS
Johnson Dental. Attached to this promotion are two sample pieces from each firm as well as a list of projects that each firm has done, and a résumé of key personnel at each firm. Both companies have proven they can put together a

mailer/pass-out piece that would effectively promote all five companies.

PARTNERSHIP PROPOSALS

Gannet Sales. French Mountain's stores have been in business four or more years and Gannet has been successfully supplying smoothie/soft yogurt equipment for 18 months, more than enough experience to launch a successful partnership on smoothie/soft yogurt sales.

Chapter 5
Targeted Message: Adjust to Client Circumstances

S
ome companies submit similar proposals to many potential clients. Clients want to receive proposals that are geared to their needs and will feel that a standard proposal just doesn't meet their specific situation. You need to be sure that any proposal you write at least appears to be specifically geared to the client's circumstances. Proposal writers want to build on a company's past success and state that the prospect's situation is just like a project the company did for another client. However, never say that you've modified the proposal you did for that client to fit the current prospect's need.

Power Paragraph

Elements of the Power Paragraph

- **First goal:** State that the client has special needs or unique circumstances.
- **Second goal:** Explain how the proposal is unique for the client.
- **Conclusion:** State that the proposal's unique features will produce the best solution for the client.

Sample Power Paragraph

This power paragraph is for Esthetics Plus (full-service supplier of skin care products). Esthetics Plus's market niche is spas and salons in California and Arizona that employ professional estheticians. This is a six-month proposal to help start up and run skin therapy departments for Renewal Spas and Salons in Northern California. The proposal envisions training professional estheticians and a department manager so that they can take over and run the program independently. This is an integrated project proposal.

Renewal Spas and Salons targets very high-income customers and wants to use its professional esthetician department as a key tool to encourage frequent visits. The department should offer services to encourage quarterly visits at a minimum and offer services that, though expensive, provide dramatic benefits. *[First goal: state that the client has special needs or unique circumstances.]* To meet this goal, this proposal includes adding several services pioneered in exclusive Switzerland spas and salons that have proven popular with European royalty and high-income families. Half of the eight recommended treatments require quarterly visits. Only two other spas, one in New York and the other in Los Angeles, offer these treatments. *[Second goal: explain how the proposal is unique for the client.]* Along with a high-ambience environment, the unique treatments offer the ideal solution to generate repeat, profitable visits from Renewal Spas and Salons' targeted customers. *[Conclusion: state that the proposal's unique features will produce the best solution for the client.]*

Applicable Proposal Sections

Letter Proposal

   4. Approach

Formal Proposal

   1d. Executive Summary—Approach
   2. Scope of the Work
   3. Initial Analysis

First Goal: State That the Client Has Special Needs or Unique Circumstances

OUTSIDE PROJECT PROPOSALS

PokerMania.com (Web site with poker instruction, supplies, accessories, and news on upcoming tournaments by state). *Proposal for the soon-to-open Washington County Race Track Card Room to offer an interactive computer poker course, with a simulated game environment, to enable new players to learn how to play the five types of card games offered by the card room.*

The closest card room to the Washington County Race Track is 400 miles away and most of the targeted customers in Washington County have never played in a casino-type card room or extensively played Texas Hold 'Em and other card room games.

INTEGRATED PROJECT PROPOSALS

MediaTile Smart Signs (signs with wireless connectivity for retail stores, enabling stores to change in-store signs from the office). *Proposal to work together with Supermarket IT Consulting to introduce MediaTile Smart Signs' system in 38 Bob's Produce grocery stores in the Colorado, Wyoming, and Montana markets.*

Supermarket IT Consulting has been Bob's Produce IT supplier for seven years. This proposal calls for MediaTile to license its technology to Supermarket IT and to work cooperatively for training and installation start-up assistance.

ONGOING SERVICE PROPOSALS

City Course Catering (exclusive rights to staging events, primarily weddings and rehearsal dinners, in two 1920s-era golf course clubhouses). *Proposal to Taylor Kellogg for hosting monthly anniversary and award lunches and for catering banquets for all employees in July and December.*

Taylor Kellogg has obtained four major contracts for 2005 and 2006, which requires extraordinary extra efforts from its employees. To show appreciation, Taylor Kellogg wants to have many special events at prestigious locations at which awards and bonuses will be handed out to employees during the last half of 2005, 2006, and the first half of 2007.

JOINT COOPERATION PROPOSALS

Johnson Dental (three dentists and two hygienists serving new housing developments). *Proposal for a joint marketing and mailing campaign to the Briarwood and Oakwood committees, to be presented to Briarwood Veterinarians, Curves exercise club for women, KinderCare Learning Center, and Spectacles Opticians shop.*

Briarwood and Oakwood are fast-growing neighborhoods and all five businesses have been open for less than six months. New residents might consider returning to their old neighborhoods for dental care, veterinary services, health clubs, child care, and optical needs; all five businesses want to make a special push, on a limited budget, to encourage residents to give them a try.

PARTNERSHIP PROPOSALS

Gannet Sales (supplies and services a complete line of soft-serve frozen yogurt and smoothie equipment). *Proposal to French Mountain Bakeries for starting up and running smoothie and soft yogurt stations in 18 French Mountain stores.*

French Mountain is a struggling new coffee-and-pastry chain that closes at 2:00 p.m. for lack of business. French Mountain cannot afford to purchase smoothie equipment in the hope that the new item will allow the stores to stay open through afternoon and evening hours.

Second Goal: Explain How the Proposal Is Unique for the Client

OUTSIDE PROJECT PROPOSALS

PokerMania. This project is to prepare an interactive training site that can be used on eight training computers in the entrance to the card room. The training site will have four levels, from beginner to advanced, to help people feel more comfortable playing. The first two levels for beginners are specially designed for Washington County and will feature game tables as they exist in the actual card room and will have over 100 practice hands and three strategies that can be played with each hand.

INTEGRATED PROJECT PROPOSALS

MediaTile Smart Signs. MediaTile will assign two people, specialized in software and installation, to Supermarket IT's location for a period of three months to work to ensure that the installation at Bob's Produce locations goes smoothly as well as to provide thorough training courses for Supermarket IT personnel.

ONGOING SERVICE PROPOSALS

City Course Catering. City Course Catering offers several deluxe banquet settings for both luncheons and bigger events, and it will bring in chefs from Chez Paul and Ristorante Italiano to prepare special meals for these occasions to offer employees a unique high-value meal. Media service will also be available for presentations and videos.

JOINT COOPERATION PROPOSALS

Johnson Dental. Rydall Advertising is offering to prepare special pop-up promotional material that can be mailed out or distributed in each office. The pieces cost more than any one office can spend, but are less than three times the cost of a typical advertising flier.

PARTNERSHIP PROPOSALS

Gannet Sales. Gannet has arranged for financing to put smoothie machines into 18 locations and will supply all smoothie ingredients in return for 70% of smoothie revenue. If the new offering is not successful, Gannet will take the equipment back and sell it to other customers.

Conclusion: State That the Proposal's Unique Features Will Produce the Best Solution for the Client

OUTSIDE PROJECT PROPOSALS

PokerMania. The goal is to get people to try playing; the in-depth instruction at many different levels offers the best solution for all levels of players to get involved in at least the $1 tables.

INTEGRATED PROJECT PROPOSALS

MediaTile Smart Signs. The dedication of two employees provides Supermarket IT the best solution for fully training its staff and for executing error-free installation and start-up.

ONGOING SERVICE PROPOSALS

City Course Catering. The right atmosphere, special meals, and a separate location for only Taylor Kellogg employees is a solution that will demonstrate Taylor Kellogg's appreciation of its employees' extra efforts to meet this short-term load of extra business.

JOINT COOPERATION PROPOSALS

Johnson Dental. A joint program encourages each firm's current customers to try out a new business and it also provides a high-impact mailing piece. A joint program offers the best solution for all five companies to effectively promote their businesses to their growing target market at a reasonable cost.

PARTNERSHIP PROPOSALS

Gannet Sales. This partnership arrangement allows French

Mountain to explore whether or not a smoothie and soft yogurt station will allow it to profitably stay open until 9:00 p.m. while risking only the labor costs at its 18 sites. This is an ideal solution to test the concept without significant risk.

Chapter 6
Deliverables:
Fit the Client's Goals

Deliverables (which are the work, report, or other tangible items you furnish the client) are the trickiest part of any proposal: they give clients assurance that the project will produce tangible results but you don't want to overpromise deliverables or you won't be able to provide the contract at a competitive cost. Since you don't know what the competition will do, I believe you have to list first the deliverable most important to the client and then the other deliverables you offer as additional options. That way if the cost is too high you leave the client the option of asking for a revised deliverable.

Power Paragraph

Elements of the Power Paragraph

- **First goal:** State what the client has requested as deliverables.

- **Second goal:** List what additional deliverables will be provided.

- **Conclusion:** Explain how the deliverables meet the client's goal.

Sample Power Paragraph

This power paragraph is for Closed Caption Theatre Technology (CCTT), a company that provides closed captioning equipment to theaters for a monthly fee. The company is proposing to the Carmike Theaters' Northeast Region Director, to provide a funding request to a major group that provides accessibility funding for entertainment complexes (an outside project proposal).

CCTT will deliver to Carmike Theaters Northeast Region a complete proposal for partially funding three-year service contracts of CCTT systems at 30% of Carmike's cinemas. *[First goal: state what the client has requested as deliverables.]* CCTT will also provide a complete fundraising plan and a list of funding sources and provide written response to inquiries from those sources. *[Second goal: list what additional deliverables will be provided.]* The plan, proposal, and follow-up should produce funding for at least 50% of the costs of Carmike's CCTT systems. *[Conclusion: explain how the deliverables meet the client's goal.]*

Applicable Proposal Sections

Letter Proposal
   6. Deliverables

Formal Proposal
   1c. Executive Summary—Client's or Partner's Goals
   9c. Implementation—Deliverables

First Goal: State What the Client Has Requested as Deliverables

Proposals succeed by meeting client's expectations. Most clients have a firm idea of what they expect in your proposal and they probably have a firm expectation of what they expect the deliverables to be. Don't start a proposal until you find out what the customer's expectations are during your preliminary meetings. Start your power paragraph on deliverables by matching or exceeding the customer's expectations on deliverables.

OUTSIDE PROJECT PROPOSALS

Raphael's Medical (offers medical information in Spanish and an extensive list of providers with a staff who speak Spanish). *Proposal to provide a marketing report to the East Side Clinic regarding Hispanics in its market area, how their medical needs are being serviced, and what action the clinic could take to increase its share of this business.*

Raphael's Medical will deliver to the East Side Clinic a comprehensive, 40- to 50-page marketing report, including a situation analysis and an action plan.

INTEGRATED PROJECT PROPOSALS

Advantage Marketing Specialties (advertising promotion specialties). *Proposal to work with the sponsors of a golf tournament to select giveaway prizes for big donors.*

As a member of the promotional products selection committee, Advantage Marketing will deliver cost quotes and samples on premiums requested by the tournament organizers as well as suggest alternative premiums.

ONGOING SERVICE PROPOSALS

Denny's Auto Repair (four-bay auto repair garage). *Proposal to Bostrom Transportation Services to provide repair service for its fleet of 10 coaches.*

Denny's guarantees an average repair turnaround of less than 48 hours and four-hour pickup of downed buses within 50 miles of Bostrom headquarters.

JOINT COOPERATION PROPOSALS

Innovative Tooling (coordinates with an alliance of custom tool manufacturers to provide any required custom tool). *Proposal to Specialty Steel, a steel distributor to the machining industry, and Roberts Tool and Die, which specializes in fixtures and jigs for custom manufacturing jobs, to sponsor a series of educational seminars on custom jobs for the airline industry using Inconel, a high-strength nickel-chromium-iron alloy.*

Innovative Tooling will coordinate presentations from eight tooling experts for a training seminar sponsored by Innovative Tooling, Specialty Steel, and Roberts Tool and Die. Innovative will arrange for demonstrations from the six leading machining center manufacturers.

PARTNERSHIP PROPOSALS

Wall Concepts (manufacturer of faux painting sponges). *Proposal to Valspar Paints, a manufacturer of glazing paints, to offer a faux painting center, with instructions, to major home centers on the East Coast, with sales going through Valspar but profits from sales through the faux painting centers to be split 75/25, with Valspar receiving the 75% share.*

Deliverables: Fit the Client's Goals

Wall Concepts will deliver to the partnership immediate stock of 40,000 faux painting sponges and a commitment to supply an additional 120,000 in calendar year 2007. In addition, Wall Concepts will provide proposed sales flyers and store displays for the partnership marketing team.

Second Goal: List What Additional Deliverables Will Be Provided

After matching the client's expectation, you should try to offer additional deliverables that will also contribute toward meeting the client's goal. This will separate you from the competition. Another advantage of extra deliverables, as mentioned before, is that if your price is higher than the client's budget, the client might come back and ask for a quote without the extra deliverables.

OUTSIDE PROJECT PROPOSALS

Raphael's Medical. Included with the plan is a PowerPoint presentation that can be presented to the East Side Clinic Board and a specific action plan related to the marketing report for each of the six key clinic employees involved with plan activities.

INTEGRATED PROJECT PROPOSALS

Advantage Marketing Specialties. Advantage will also obtain a list of promotional items for each of the 10 preceding tournaments so the committee avoids picking promotional giveaways similar to ones that sponsors have already received.

ONGOING SERVICE PROPOSALS

Denny's Auto Repair. Denny's will also work with bus scheduling to perform preventative maintenance at times when doing so won't force curtailed service.

JOINT COOPERATION PROPOSALS

Innovative Tooling. Innovative Tooling will also coordinate the customer lists of the three firms and each firm will receive a joint contact list for Texas, Oklahoma, and Kansas.

PARTNERSHIP PROPOSALS

Wall Concepts. Wall Concepts will also provide results from a marketing survey of 445 end users and home stores, which can be used by the partnership's marketing group.

Conclusion: Explain How the Deliverables Meet the Client's Goal

Deliverables are only a means to an end; what counts is meeting the client's goals. You want to tie the two together because the client can always decide to do nothing. Always reinforce that your proposal will meet a key client goal, in order to encourage the client to move ahead and to set yourself above the competition.

OUTSIDE PROJECT PROPOSALS

Raphael's Medical. The plan, presentation, and specific action plans should convince the East Side Clinic's board that the proposed $75,000 will successfully launch the clinic's Hispanic community development program.

INTEGRATED PROJECT PROPOSALS

Advantage Marketing Specialties. Starting early, the tournament will be able to select memorable, unique gifts that will provide a positive impact on sponsors.

ONGOING SERVICE PROPOSALS

Denny's Auto Repair. Quick service and a complete preventative maintenance program will allow Bostrom's to achieve 92% or better fleet utilization.

JOINT COOPERATION PROPOSALS

Innovative Tooling. The joint seminars with a strong presentation by industry's leaders will attract a high number of participants from local machine shops and offer all three companies an excellent chance to promote their products and services to their target customers.

PARTNERSHIP PROPOSALS

Wall Concepts. A partnership enables Valspar and Wall Concepts to offer a complete faux painting product solution, along with instruction kits and faux painting helper Web sites that makes both companies' products more attractive to both consumers and home centers.

Chapter 7
Cost: Deliver
High Value

ost is always a major issue with proposals—potential clients need to feel your proposal is worth the money, lower-priced competitors often bid against you, and clients may not have enough money in their budget to pay for the proposal. I believe you should write every proposal as if there will be a lower-price proposal presented and you need to counter that lower-cost proposal by demonstrating that your proposal delivers extra value for the price to the potential client or partner.

You sell value three ways in a proposal: one, you closely meet the client's needs and goals; two, you provide extra features that help the client meet its goals; and three, you have the expertise to meet the client's needs. You've made these points in earlier power points, but you want to state them again with the price to reinforce that your proposal is an exceptional value for your prospect.

Power Paragraph

Elements of the Power Paragraph

- **First goal:** State the cost of the proposal.

- **Second goal:** List the client's expectations regarding goals.
- **Third goal:** Mention the extras that exceed expectations.
- **Conclusion:** Explain that your proposal is a perfect fit.

Sample Power Paragraph

This power paragraph is for Jetboil Personal Cooking System (outdoors complete cooking system, with cooking vessel, flame, and fuel source contained in a patented flux ring for fast and safe cooking in any conditions). The company is presenting a joint cooperation proposal to Adventure Foods, manufacturer of instant backpack food, Wilderness Dining, manufacturer of backpacking cooking equipment, and Mary Jane Farms, manufacturer of high-protein backpacking snacks, proposing that the companies join together to offer a complete one-week cooking pack for backpackers, to be offered for sale by Backpacking Adventures.

Each company's costs will be under $2,500, which includes the cost of preparing a joint reorder file for the individual components of the cooking pack, the costs of preparing a total cooking pack Web page for Backpacking Adventures, the costs of sample cooking packs for trade shows, and the costs of setting up an electronic data exchange so sales revenue is split evenly. *[First goal: state the cost of the proposal.]* Each partner wants to increase its sales exposure to new backpackers in a cost-effective way. Backpacking Adventures, which caters to novice backpackers with trip information, offers a Web site praised in media publications that generates a high number of visitors. *[Second goal: list the client's expectations regarding goals.]* As a bonus to participating companies, Backpacking Adventures will display the cooking pack, its contents, and its components reorder form at the over 25 yearly consumer backpacking shows it attends. [Third goal: mention the extras that exceed expectations.] Working together, the companies offer a valuable tool to Backpacking Adventures and in return Backpacking Adventures will offer to the companies low-cost, positive exposure for their product lines. *[Conclusion: explain that your proposal is a perfect fit.]*

Applicable Proposal Sections

Letter Proposal
   7. Costs

Formal Proposal
   1f. Executive Summary—Pricing and Cost-Benefit Analysis
   7. Pricing

First Goal: State the Cost of the Proposal

People receiving proposals don't like to dig for the proposal costs. Be straightforward and up front in cost sections of the plan. Also include a cost chart if the proposal contains several options or cost components.

OUTSIDE PROJECT PROPOSALS

Schuylkill Valley Medical (offers emergency medical training). *Proposal to Airco Industrial for training on-site responders for special procedures related to cryogenics health emergencies.*

The cost of a two-week training course at an Airco Industrial site for 15 people will be $50,000, which includes cryogenics training certification for Schuylkill's instructors.

INTEGRATED PROJECT PROPOSALS

CottaZilk (produces a new type of fabric, a hybrid of silk and cotton, with the look and feel of silk and the cleaning ease of cotton). *Proposal to Carolyn's Fabrics to create a special version of CottaZilk for a special line of formal evening wear.*

The cost of working together with Carolyn's Fabrics to create a new type of fabric for evening wear will be $20,000.

ONGOING SERVICE PROPOSALS

Anesthesiology Billing (billing and insurance claims service). *Proposal to HealthWest to take over its billing and insurance claims for anesthesiology services.*

Anesthesiology Billing's monthly fee to HealthWest will be $14,000 per month.

JOINT COOPERATION PROPOSALS

ZZ's Organic Restaurant (serves organically grown fruits and vegetables and pasture-raised, hormone- and antibiotic-free meat). *Proposal to two other organic restaurants and a chain of four co-op grocery stores to produce an organic food newsletter.*

Each participant in the program will need to pay $1,250 per month to prepare and print the newsletter. Later some ad content may be included, which could cut costs.

PARTNERSHIP PROPOSALS

BankIntelligence (provides current money market rates, national loan rates, and federal fund rates to banks and investment firms). *Proposal to Virtual Due Diligence (electronic storage of all documents pertinent to any business deal, but especially mergers and acquisitions, with a site that enables all parties to access data simultaneously, rather than each party in succession) for the two companies to join together into one company to share software programming and researcher costs.*

The total cost of joining BankIntelligence and Virtual Due Diligence is $30,000 for legal fees, the cost of new shares, and the breaking of a lease. The total is to be split between the two companies, with each absorbing $15,000 in costs.

Second Goal: List the Client's Expectations Regarding Goals

Effective proposal writers think in terms of their client's goals and expectations for results. Those are the top two items on the prospective client's agenda. When listing the price or proposal costs, always tie them back to the client's goals and then show that the proposal meets or exceeds the client's expectations.

If you can't meet the client's expectations, don't make the common mistake of listing what you can do, which is an effort to control the client's expectations. The prospect will just be disappointed in your proposal and will be unlikely to buy. Instead, before doing the proposal, tell the prospective client you can't meet the expectation and why and see if it is willing to modify those expectations. That way the client will get a proposal that meets its revised expectations.

OUTSIDE PROJECT PROPOSALS

Schuylkill Valley Medical. This proposal is for a course that provides all the normal first-responder training but also adds one week of training for immediate response for cryogenics emergencies, including burns and asphyxiation tissue damage.

INTEGRATED PROJECT PROPOSALS

CottaZilk. Carolyn's Fabrics' goal is to have an exotic new look, incorporating fabric and design. Dedicating a fabric line and textile chemist to Carolyn's will allow Carolyn's the ultimate flexibility in trying out different combinations to find the desired exotic look.

ONGOING SERVICE PROPOSALS
Anesthesiology Billing. Anesthesiology Billing will eliminate 100 hours per month of administrative work for HealthWest and will cut payment time from 90 to 45 days.

JOINT COOPERATION PROPOSALS
ZZ's Organic Restaurant. The goal of all participants is to convert initial or one-time customers into regular customers by demonstrating the long-lasting benefits of organic foods. The newsletter provides a convenient, cost-effective tool to do that.

PARTNERSHIP PROPOSALS
BankIntelligence proposal to Virtual Due Diligence. The goal for both companies in forming a partnership is to cut overhead as a percent of sales from 38% to 26%. Cutting rent and sharing resources in a partnership will generate those savings.

Third Goal: Mention the Extras That Exceed Expectations

Clients like suppliers that work extra hard for them or understand their goals and go above and beyond the clients' immediate request to help them meet those goals. If you are offering extra work or services as part of your proposal, be sure to list them here.

OUTSIDE PROJECT PROPOSALS
Schuylkill Valley Medical. Prior to the training, Schulykill Valley will receive certification as a cryogenics first-responder instructor from the Linde Institute in Germany so that training participants can receive a certified cryogenics training rating.

INTEGRATED PROJECT PROPOSALS
CottaZilk. In addition to the line and textile chemist, CottaZilk will offer a special one-day brainstorming session with the Director of R&D to lay out all the possible options.

ONGOING SERVICE PROPOSALS
Anesthesiology Billing. The proposal also calls for a software package that will eliminate over 90% of the initial input errors and raise revenue 5% to 10%.

JOINT COOPERATION PROPOSALS
ZZ's Organic Restaurant. An added plus of a newsletter is that it is a convenient tool to help current customers convince friends and family to give organic foods a try.

PARTNERSHIP PROPOSALS

BankIntelligence proposal to Virtual Due Diligence. The partnership will also have expanded resources to pursue opportunities in both target markets that the companies are not able to pursue separately.

Conclusion: Explain That Your Proposal Is a Perfect Fit

The perfect phrase to conclude your cost power paragraph simply explains why your company is the perfect solution to the client's needs. A perfect fit makes your price secondary to the performance your company is offering. That is the crucial image you want to leave with the proposal reader—confidence that you will get the job done right, which is, in the end, what produces your proposal's high value.

OUTSIDE PROJECT PROPOSALS
Schuylkill Valley Medical. As part of the proposal, Schuylkill Valley Medical will become the only certified cryogenics emergency response training firm in the U.S. That will make it a perfect fit for Airco's current and future needs to have rapid response teams at all its facilities.

INTEGRATED PROJECT PROPOSALS
CottaZilk. This proposal offers Carolyn's Fabrics the resources of CottaZilk to create what will be viewed as an innovative jump in women's formal wear.

ONGOING SERVICE PROPOSALS
Anesthesiology Billing. Anesthesiology Billing's experience and proven performance will eliminate what has become a bottleneck in HealthWest's revenue stream.

JOINT COOPERATION PROPOSALS
ZZ's Organic Restaurant. A joint newsletter promotes organic foods as a viable choice enjoyed by many consumers and cost-effectively promotes each business. It is

without a doubt the best marketing option for all of the cash-strapped participants.

PARTNERSHIP PROPOSALS

BankIntelligence proposal to Virtual Due Diligence. Both companies have similar technology platforms and their researchers are accumulating data in similar places. Those forces can be combined with minimal effort and the result will be better utilization of resources and lower costs, an ideal starting point for any partnership.

Chapter 8
Value Added: Clear
Benefits for the Customer

Proposals must meet the client's goals and expectations, but they need to do more than that. They have to show that, when complete, the proposal adds strong value for the client for its overall business operation. One of the difficulties of a proposal is that the writer is preparing a document that meets a specific need or goal for the person or department to whom or for which the proposal is directed. But your proposal doesn't stand alone. Often the company has other projects or other opportunities on which it can spend its money and the final decision for which proposals or projects to move ahead with depends on which one offers the customer the most value for the money. So your final point has to be to show that your proposal meets the immediate goal—and that it also generates high value for the customer in its overall operation. This can be more difficult to do on a specific proposal for an administrative task, such as Anesthesiology Billing's proposal to take over a medical group's anesthesiology billing and collection process, but I believe you can always find a greater good for the customer in any type of proposal.

Power Paragraph

Elements of the Power Paragraph

- **First goal:** Identify the value added beyond the proposal's immediate goals.
- **Second goal:** Explain the benefit of the added value.
- **Conclusion:** State how that benefit leads to future opportunities.

Sample Power Paragraph

This power paragraph is for Jetboil Personal Cooking System (outdoors complete cooking system, with cooking vessel, flame, and fuel source contained in a patented flux ring for fast and safe cooking in any conditions). The company is presenting a joint cooperation proposal to Adventure Foods, manufacturer of instant backpack food, Wilderness Dining, manufacturer of backpacking cooking equipment, and Mary Jane Farms, manufacturer of high-protein backpacking snacks, proposing that the companies join together to offer a complete one-week cooking pack for backpackers to be offered for sale by Backpacking Adventures.

> Besides the immediate sales potential of this program, being involved with Backpacking Adventures will help establish the brand names of all company participants. *[First goal: identify the value added beyond the proposal's immediate goals.]* Consumer brand recognition will help each company in its efforts to increase its shelf space in major backpacking retailers. *[Second goal: explain the benefit of the added value.]* More involvement with retailers and major backpacking promoters like Backpacking Adventures will help the companies keep abreast of market trends and allow them to become

the market innovators. *[Conclusion: state how that benefit leads to future opportunities.]*

Applicable Proposal Sections

Letter Proposal
   8. Conclusion

Formal Proposal
  1d. Executive Summary—Approach
   2. Scope of the Work
   8. Cost-Benefit Analysis

First Goal: Identify the Value Added Beyond the Proposal's Immediate Goals

The value-added points of your proposal are related to the benefits that will come to the company long after the project is completed. Think ahead six months to three years and decide what additional benefits the prospect will receive after implementing your proposal. Those changes are the value-added points that you should identify here.

OUTSIDE PROJECT PROPOSALS

Schuylkill Valley Medical (offers emergency medical training). *Proposal to Airco Industrial for training on-site responders for special procedures related to cryogenics health emergencies.*

After training, Airco personnel will be the only force in the country with in-depth cryogenics training, and Airco will be able to offer its customers access to its emergency response staff.

INTEGRATED PROJECT PROPOSALS

CottaZilk (produces a new type of fabric, a hybrid of silk and cotton, with the look and feel of silk and the cleaning ease of cotton). Proposal to Carolyn's Fabrics to create a special version of CottaZilk for a special line of formal evening wear.

This is the first known industry joint fabric/designer project. The project coordination offers a new dimension into dress design.

ONGOING SERVICE PROPOSALS

Anesthesiology Billing (billing and insurance claims service). *Proposal to HealthWest to take over its billing and insur-*

ance claims for anesthesiology services.

Improved billing procedures can be the first step for HealthWest to free up its administrative staff to concentrate on more important aspects of the business, including establishing relationships with additional doctors and clinics that are currently using other hospitals.

JOINT COOPERATION PROPOSALS

ZZ's Organic Restaurant (serves organically grown fruits and vegetables and pasture-raised, hormone- and antibiotic-free meat). *Proposal to two other organic restaurants and a chain of four co-op grocery stores to produce an organic food newsletter.*

A newsletter can begin to modify mainstream Columbus, Ohio, consumers' view of organic food as being part of a fringe, far-left lifestyle.

PARTNERSHIP PROPOSALS

BankIntelligence (provides current money market rates, national loan rates, and federal fund rates to banks and investment firms). *Proposal to Virtual Due Diligence (electronic storage of all documents pertinent to any business deal, but especially mergers and acquisitions, with a site that enables all parties to access data simultaneously, rather than each party in succession) for the two companies to join together into one company to share software programming and researcher costs.*

Besides cutting costs, a partnership will reinforce each brand's image as a site for sophisticated financial information.

Second Goal: Explain the Benefit of the Added Value

Your proposal solves a problem or meets a need, but probably so do all the other proposals the prospective customer will receive. You need to separate yourself from the competition. One way to do that is to mention the benefits of your proposal for the company overall, benefits that will allow the company to improve some aspect of its business.

OUTSIDE PROJECT PROPOSALS

Schuylkill Valley Medical. Customers' access to emergency response is a differentiating benefit for Airco, which may be able to become at least a secondary supplier to customers that till now have purchased only from Airco's competitors.

INTEGRATED PROJECT PROPOSALS

CottaZilk. Carolyn's Fabrics will receive significant positive media attention from the joint project, which will help launch sales for its new line.

ONGOING SERVICE PROPOSALS

Anesthesiology Billing. 15% fewer doctors are referring patients to HealthWest's hospitals today than three years ago. Minimizing billing bottlenecks will allow staff to concentrate on meeting doctors' needs, which responds to doctors' number-one complaint, that HealthWest is not responsive to their specialized needs.

JOINT COOPERATION PROPOSALS

ZZ's Organic Restaurant. Changing the fringe image of organic food will help it attract more patrons.

PARTNERSHIP PROPOSALS

BankIntelligence proposal to Virtual Due Diligence.
Both parties have recently established their market and to date no competitors have emerged. An enhanced image as a source of savvy information for the financial community should help the partnership delay competition until the companies are established market leaders.

Conclusion: State How That Benefit Leads to Future Opportunities

Cost, sales, margins, and administrative tasks are the day-to-day activities that proposals often center on. But companies act on opportunities to substantially increase their business. Listing opportunities improves your chances of impressing the prospect, especially the management, and your chances of landing the contract.

OUTSIDE PROJECT PROPOSALS
Schuylkill Valley Medical. If Airco proceeds with a nationwide training program, it will be in a good position to become the preferred supplier to many or even most major cryogenics customers.

INTEGRATED PROJECT PROPOSALS
CottaZilk. Longer term, the project conveys the image that Carolyn's is an innovator in design, a reputation that will add to its brand image and increase attention to its new lines for years to come.

ONGOING SERVICE PROPOSALS
Anesthesiology Billing. As HealthWest addresses its image problems, it will be able to re-establish itself as the market leader in meeting the needs of private physicians.

JOINT COOPERATION PROPOSALS
ZZ's Organic Restaurant. While organic foods will probably never be the preferred choice of the average consumer, all the participants in this newsletter project would benefit if just 10% of the consumers in our market routinely ate organic food.

PARTNERSHIP PROPOSALS

BankIntelligence proposal to Virtual Due Diligence.
While competition is sure to develop as the partnership succeeds, both brands should be able to build up the researching and computing power to continue to hold at least a 50% market share.

Part Two

Perfect Phrases for Business Plans

The Business Plan Scorecard

Many business plan readers are bankers, investors, or consultants who read dozens if not hundreds of plans per year. Obviously they need a method of judging one plan against another, and I've found that the 10 points listed below are the ones that most investors and bankers look for when deciding if a company has a great business concept and is worth investing in. The book describes perfect phrases and power paragraphs that deal with the 10 items on the business plan scorecard. My goal is to give you phrases to choose from that allow you to write a power paragraph for each item on the scorecard so you will convince readers yours is a business in which to invest.

The executive summary section of the plan and the business plan format I've included in this book closely follow the scorecard. Use your perfect phrases and power paragraphs in the executive summary and then again as the lead paragraph in the introduction portion of each section of the plan. This section of the book contains two examples from seven types of businesses so you have plenty of perfect phrases to express your approach when writing your plan. I've tried to offer this wide range of business examples so you as the reader can find the right one for you.

One cautionary note: businesses have radically different strategies, from being a technology leader to being a low cost supplier. Your plan has to fit your strategy. Chapter 1 offers a list of common business strategies. Before writing your plan decide which basic business strategy your company follows. Be sure to include phrases that support your business strategy. Each chapter offers phrases that will help you emphasize your business strategy as you prepare these power paragraphs. These phrases will help readers of your plan realize you have a clear understanding of why you chose your business strategy and that you understand what steps are needed to successfully implement that strategy. The following lists the different components of the business scorecard coverd in this book and the chapters in which these items are covered.

1. **Customers:** Great Ones Make Great Businesses (Chapter 3)
2. **Market Drivers:** The Building Blocks of Success (Chapter 4)
3. **Market Size:** Offer Plenty of Room for Growth (Chapter 5)
4. **Market Niche:** A Space That Produces Profits (Chapter 6)
5. **Competitive Advantage:** How You Stand Out (Chapter 7)
6. **Margins:** Predicting Business Strength (Chapter 8)
7. **Start-Up Costs:** Justified by the Market Opportunity (Chapter 9)
9. **Founder Financing:** Show Commitment to the Business (Chapter 10)

Chapter 9
Business Strategies

mentioned in the introduction to this part that you'll find in each chapter key messages that plans must deliver for seven typical business strategies. I've found that many first-time plan writers are confused about the terms used to describe common strategies. Those strategies are listed below along with examples of different businesses that follow that strategy. These will give you a better idea of which strategy is applicable for your business. Decide which strategy your business is following and be sure to include the key messages for that strategy in your plan.

Common Strategies

1. Market Maker. A company that introduces a new concept, not on the market before. The Palm Pilot, the first personal digital assistant (PDA), is an example of a market-maker product. Other examples include:

- **Product:** Big Bertha, the first oversized golf club with a "whippy" shaft graphite, created a new category for long-distance golf drivers.

- **Retail:** Young Rembrandt and Kidz Art pioneered the concept of art classes and supplies for kids from three to 12.
- **Service:** Jiffy Lube pioneered the concept of the 15-minute oil change.
- **Professional:** LASIK (Laser-Assisted *in Situ* Keratomileusis) surgery emerged in the late 1990s as a new way to correct vision.

2. Market Enabler. This is a service, retailer, or product that helps a new trend in the market or helps a market maker product expand its application. Scrapbook stores are market enablers for the scrapbook industry. Other examples include:

- **Product:** The Stowaway keyboard, a computer keyboard for PDAs that folds into four sections to fit into a suit pocket, enabling the market for PDAs.
- **Retail:** Renovator's Supply, Inc., a chain of hardware stores that provides a full line of supplies for people who want to renovate older homes, enabling the market for "urban homesteading."
- **Service:** Whole home ventilation, a service of HVAC dealers that brings fresh air into airtight new homes so the air doesn't go stale, helps the sale of super-insulated houses.
- **Distribution:** HealthSTAR Communications, Inc. provides independent, outsourced pharmaceutical marketing and sales services to biotech pharmaceutical companies, offering a reasonable cost path to market for small to mid-size biotech companies.

3. Technology Leader. A company with advanced technology that provides a benefit to customers. Wireless Zone®, a retail store with all things wireless for home and business networks, including service and technical support, provides customers with the best available technology.

- **Product:** Select Comfort Corporation, which produces beds that allow each person to adjust the firmness of his or her side of the bed.
- **Retail:** Fry's Electronics, Inc., specializes in having all the latest high-tech gear for technology enthusiasts.
- **Service:** SIRIUS Radio created new technology to launch its satellite radio service.
- **Distribution:** McKesson Corporation sells health-care management products to doctors, nursing homes, and others and has a major market advantage because of advanced software (for the industry) and management controls that make its error rate 10% of the industry average.

4. Niche Marketer. A niche market is a subset of a bigger market for customers with specific needs. People who use drycleaners three to four times a week are a niche of the overall dry cleaning market. 1-800-DryClean, LLC, Dry Cleaning To-Your-Door®, and Pressed4Time, Inc. all target this market with pick-up and delivery dry cleaning. Other examples are:

- **Product:** River Park, Inc. supplies electronic sound and other products such as OnStar (an electronic emergency communication system) to RV manufacturers.
- **Retail:** Curves International, Inc. fitness salons, exercise clubs where all women can feel comfortable—no men, no mirrors, and no make-up.
- **Service:** Smile Centers, a business run by dental hygienists who provide teeth cleaning and whitening for people who demand a perfect smile.

■ **Service:** Investology, a firm that provides research on small-capitalization stocks ignored by market analysts from large firms. Target customers are small to mid-size mutual funds whose managers want to hold a broader variety of stocks than large funds.

5. Customer Solution. Customers buy products or services to achieve a result. One business strategy is to provide customers a total solution. Wireless Zone, mentioned above as a technology leader, is also a customer solution. Another example is lawn care services that create a perfect lawn by providing services from fertilizing to mowing. Other examples are:

■ **Product:** Both Norton (Symantec Corporation) and McAfee, Inc. anti-virus programs offer complete solutions to customers' worries about computer security.

■ **Retail:** Trader Joe's, a complete grocery store that sells only heart-healthy foods. ISold It, LLC stores provide every service for an individual to sell a product on eBay.

■ **Service:** MSC (Medical Services Company) provides one-stop medical rehab services to workers' compensation patients on behalf of insurance carriers offering better service to patients and better cost control to the insurance carriers.

■ **Service:** The Maids, Molly Maids, and Merry Maids keep a house clean and solve the problem of finding a reliable maid who comes every week.

6. Performance Enhancer. These companies provide a product or service that just works better for customers. A hand-held scanner for breast cancer is less invasive than traditional mammograms. Papa Murphy's Pizza, besides costing less, offers an easy way for buyers to have "hot from the oven" pizza. Other examples are:

- **Product:** The Java Jacket is a piece of cardboard with "patented embossed nubbins" that fits around a paper coffee cup so it is not too hot to hold.
- **Retail:** Starbucks Coffee, better coffee in a more relaxing environment. Quiznos offers toasted subs as an improvement over Subway's more traditional subs.
- **Service:** Home Instead Senior Care, Comfort Keepers, and Visiting Angels all provide routine senior home care, a big improvement over once-or-twice visits from a nurse or weekly visits from family members.
- **Distribution:** Gustave A. Larson is a heating, ventilation, and air conditioning (HVAC) distributor who sells products to HVAC dealers. Extra services that other distributors don't offer include dealer development leaders. These are marketing people who help dealers upgrade their business and technical experts whom dealers can call when installation problems arise.

7. Efficiency Improver. Wal-Mart succeeds by discovering methods of cutting costs and then passing those savings on to the consumer. Other examples are:

- **Product:** Dell Computer has streamlined its production and distribution process to offer sustainable lower pricing. Stuart Energy has a lower-cost technology for producing hydrogen from electrolysis (decomposing water into hydrogen and oxygen).
- **Retail:** Flowerama floral centers are stand-alone flower stores, with a large inventory and parking, offering easy-in-

and-out access to buyers looking for a quick gift. The ease of shopping increases volume and lowers costs.

- **Service:** Larry's Sharpening offers low-cost sharpening services to dog clippers with specialized, dedicated equipment and a mobile unit that sharpens clippers at the dog groomer's location, which also allows the groomer to have fewer clippers.
- **Professional:** Prescott & Pearson, P.A. is a law firm in New Brighton, Minnesota, that specializes in low-cost bankruptcy services, allowing it to cut the price of services over traditional law firms.

Chapter 10
Typical Format:
Matching Expectations

Business plan writers want to convey that the company has professional know-how, a special opportunity, and a sound business concept. First impressions count; the look of your plan and its format are important. If you've never done a plan before, attend a venture conference to see what other plans look like. You can find venture conferences at www.acve.com, the Web site for *American Ventures Magazine* and at www.angel-investors-news.com, under "opportunities for entrepreneurs." You might also be able to view plans at your local Small Business Development Center (SBDC), which you can locate at www.sba.gov/sbdc. If you're not confident of the business plan format after seeing several plans, the preface lists several business plan books that include detailed information on how to format a business plan.

Business Plan Format

The business plan format is not rigid. You can make some adjustments to it to better reflect your business, but you don't want to stray too far from the typical format or you might create the impression in the minds of readers that you are inexperienced.

1. Executive Summary. This is the most crucial part of a business plan. The purpose is to create enough interest for readers to go on and read the rest of the plan. The summary incorporates all the key elements of the plan and most of the perfect business plan phrases will be both in the executive summary and later in the plan.

Sections

a. Description, including the name of the company, when it was founded, the structure (i.e., sole proprietorship, corporation, partnership, or other), and the location

b. Business concept or description

c. Target customer group and key need or desire (Point 1 on Scorecard)

d. Target market and market drivers (Point 2 on Scorecard)

e. Market size and niche (Points 3 and 4 on Scorecard)

f. Key advantage (Point 5 on Scorecard)

g. Proprietary advantages (Point 6 on Scorecard)

h. Management team (Point 7 on Scorecard)

i. Description of operations

j. Sales history/projections/margins. (Point 8 on scorecard)

k. Start-up costs (Point 9 on Scorecard)

l. Capitalization or financing plan. (Point 10 on Scorecard)

2. Target Customers. A successful business has identified and can narrowly define a target customer group that has a need or desire for the company's product or service. (Point 1 on Scorecard)

Key Points
  a. Customer characteristics including how many and how they can be identified
  b. Customers' needs and desires as they relate to the company's product or service: what they need or desire and how each need or desire has been identified
  c. Customers' current response to their needs and why that current response isn't adequate

3. Target Markets. A great target market is established, easy to penetrate, not overcrowded, and reached through effective distribution networks.
Key Points
  a. Market drivers (Point 2 on Scorecard)
  b. Distribution channels
  c. Market size (Point 3 on Scorecard)
  d. Market niche (Point 4 on Scorecard)

4. Product, Service, or Concept. The best product, service, or retail store concepts offer a unique approach with a significant benefit that is easy for customers, investors, and banks to understand.
Key Points
  a. Product description
  b. Customers' needs or desires and how the company's product or services addresses those needs or desires
  c. Listing of specific advantages of the product for customers
  d. Explanations of proposed investment and how it will impact product and service

5. Key Advantage. Great business concepts offer a significant advantage in an area that is important to the customer or the distribution channel. This could be a product, marketing, or service advantage but it should have just one strong point. (Point 5 on Scorecard)

Key Points

a. Customers' priorities when related to the product, service, or retail store

b. Explain how your product meets customers' key priorities

c. Explain your proprietary advantages or intellectual property protection (Point 6 on Scorecard)

6. Competition. Competitors include both direct competitors, (companies with similar products) and indirect competitors (companies that customers buy from to achieve the same objective). For Jiffy Lube, for example, Valvoline Instant Oil Change is a direct competitor, while auto repair chains like Car-X, tire retailers like Tires Plus, and car dealerships that also offer oil changes are indirect competitors.

Key Points

a. Pricing/feature analysis

b. Performance against key customer criteria

c. Customer's brand preferences

d. Strengths and weaknesses

7. Marketing Strategy. Great marketing strategy focuses on customer needs and low-cost effective tactics for reaching those customers, often including alliances and partnerships.

Key Points

a. A name, slogan, and positioning strategy to help customers understand your product, service, or store's benefits

   b. Pricing and gross margins

   c. Several low-cost tactics that are available for locating and selling to customers

   d. The company's established connections or alliances that will help market the product

   e. Showing that enough resources have been dedicated to marketing to hit the sales objectives

8. Company Operations. Include a short description of how the company will run. A restaurant would include location, hours, liquor availability, types of cooks or chefs, and ambience. A distributor would include warehousing, vendors, distribution costs and practices, and drop shipping or packaging requirement.
Key Points

   a. The risks are minimal; procedures are proven and costs are understood

   b. Efforts have been made to keep fixed costs as low as possible

   c. The operation plan can be implemented quickly

9. Management. Management with experience and past success is crucial. Plan evaluators know that great business concepts fail without strong management. (Point 7 on Scorecard)
Key Points

   a. Management is experienced or has access to advisors with past success

   b. Checks and balances exist, typically with a board of directors

   c. A compensation plan exists to retain key management

10. Financial Section. This section should be thorough, showing management competence. An innovative business concept should show high margins, quick profitability, and a short pay-back period (two to three years) for any investment.

Key Points

  a. The business will produce significant profits and high margins (Point 8 on Scorecard)
  b. Sufficient cash is available to support the business

11. Required. Most plans are written to raise money, either by selling stock or getting a loan. This data may eventually be presented in an equities offering document, but it typically starts in the business plan.

Key Points

  a. The projected profit stream justifies the business' capitalization (number of shares multiplied by the values of the shares) (Point 9 on Scorecard)
  b. The founders and key management have a significant investment (Point 10 on Scorecard)

Section Format

Plans do not have to be long; in fact, in my experience, long plans don't work as well as shorter plans. For most sections of the plan you should follow a simple format that includes a brief opening statement, an explanation of the situation the company faces, an explanation of the company's response, and a conclusion. The most important part of this format, by far, is the opening statement; the conclusion is of less importance. The perfect phrases in this section of the book are meant to be included in the opening parts of each section.

The following is an example of a section on *market drivers* for JBL Consulting, a company that provides a complete solution to small business's administrative support functions. This section is long enough to communicate with a reader. Any more information than this simply detracts from your efforts to explain your business.

Section 3a. Target Markets—Market Drivers

OPENING STATEMENT

The market driver behind JBL's business is that large American companies are placing greater emphasis on increasing productivity and lower costs. A focal point of that effort is to place additional burdens on their vendors for better service and support. Owners of small businesses need to concentrate on meeting those demands to succeed. Unfortunately, 50% of owners with 20 to 100 employees spend more than 50% of their time dealing with administrative tasks and don't have time to deal with customer needs. JBL's administrative services free owners from administrative tasks and allow them to concentrate on growing their businesses.

EXPLANATION OF THE MARKET DRIVER

Over 75% of large companies have implemented lean manufacturing processes, Six Sigma supply chain solutions, or just-in-time inventory ordering in the last three years. According to several surveys of small business owners, their biggest obstacle to business success is the lack of time to address key customer concerns and demands related to supply issues. Poor inventory control, slow response to changes in order patterns, and poor production planning are just a few of the problems mentioned. The result is that 45% of small business owners reported losing a major account over the past two years.

EXPLANATION FOR THE COMPANY'S BUSINESS STRATEGY

According to a survey by Small Business Development Centers, owners want administrative functions to run by themselves. But owners find the opposite happens. 65% of small companies have just one college graduate in administration, supported by two or three clerks and one accountant. The result is poor efficiency that requires time-consuming oversight by owners. JBL Consulting offers administrative support services as an alternative to hiring expensive administrative staff in order to free the owner to address marketing and customer issues.

CONCLUSION

JBL provides all-encompassing administrative services with a staff of 25, including experts in every area, shared across many companies, to offer small businesses cost-effective, efficient administrative services. JBL offers owners what they want most: time to understand their customers' needs in order to expand their business.

Chapter 11
Customers: Great Ones
Make Great Businesses

An ideal target customer group has 1) a large number of prospects who 2) are easy to locate, 3) feel the products or services offered are important to them, and 4) spend prolifically and buy repeatedly. Creating a successful business would be a snap if every group had these characteristics. Successful businesses structure their operations and marketing to create as many of these characteristics as possible for their customer group.

What Is a Power Paragraph?

Each chapter in the business plans part of this book deals with one key issue on the evaluation scorecard. You'll find it advantageous before you start on your plan to work out a power paragraph of perfect phrases that can be used for emphasis in different sections of the plan. People skim plans, so you'll find it effective to repeat elements of the power paragraph in several places, so that readers will have a better chance of capturing your key power paragraphs.

The rest of the chapter offers you the perfect phrases for power paragraphs for a variety of businesses. Each set of businesses will be used for two chapters as examples. Choose the business closest to your own as a model for your plan's power paragraphs.

Power Paragraph

Elements of the Power Paragraph

- **First goal:** Define the customer group.
- **Second goal:** Show importance and spending patterns.
- **Third goal:** Add emphasis appropriate for the business strategy.
- **Conclusion:** Restate that a large customer group needs the product or service.

Sample Power Paragraph

This power paragraph is for the product AutoV Editor, a video-editing software system that is simple to use with a relatively small file size that competes with editing software from companies like Adobe Systems, Sonic, and Pinnacle.

The AutoV Editor targets the major manufacturers of digital camcorders, cameras, and camera phones. *[First goal: define the customer group.]* The AutoV Editor's easy-to-use video editing gives potential customers a major market advantage for their products in a major, high-profit, rapidly growing consumer market. *[Second goal: show importance and spending patterns.]* Over 85% of people with digital video never edit the video into a viewable format. The major reason people don't convert is that the process takes too long and is too difficult. *[Third goal: add emphasis appropriate for the business*

> *strategy. In this case, the key emphasis on improved performance is that the market is large and unhappy with current products.]* Companies selling products that can capture video can differentiate their products and add substantially to the customer value of their products by including the AutoV Editor's software as a no- or low-cost upgrade. *[Conclusion: restate that a large customer group needs the product or service.]*

Applicable Plan Sections

You should consider adding elements of the *customer power paragraph* to these sections of the business plan.

1c. Executive Summary—Target Customer Groups

2. Target Customers

4b. Product, Service, or Concept—Customers' Needs or Desires

5a. Key Advantage—Customers' Priorities

First Goal: Define the Customer Group

Who is the target customer group? That seems simple enough, but you have two task goals: first, to clearly define the group and hopefully quantify them, and two, to show that they are viable customers. For example, if a plan were for a new restaurant in the Skokie/Evanston, Illinois area, an ineffective plan might define the target customer as couples and families with over $80,000 in annual income. A better customer definition would be "the 500 to 600 upper-income couples and families in the Skokie/Evanston area who currently eat at Martha's, Sans Souci, and Murray's Steakhouse restaurants." This definition tells readers you have a better understanding of the customers you are serving and their numbers and points out that your target customers are already spending money on businesses like yours.

LOCAL BUSINESSES

Denny's Auto Repair (a four-bay auto repair garage) is targeting an estimated 800 residents of Conshohocken who currently drive eight miles to have their cars repaired in Norristown.

Gabrielle's Gifts (a high-end gift shop for women) will open in the successful Galleria Mall in Thousands Oaks, California, targeting the 1,000-daily-average male visitors from the numerous surrounding businesses and the affluent homes in the northern San Fernando Valley.

DISTRIBUTION BUSINESSES

Advantage Marketing Specialties (advertising promotion

specialties) targets the 450 service business in Knoxville, Tennessee, that purchase calendars, magnets, and labels to help their key customers remember their names.

Innovative Tooling (coordinates with an alliance of custom tool manufacturers to provide any required custom tool) targets the 125 small custom machine shops in Texas and Oklahoma that handle the small, highly specialized machining jobs that require custom machine tooling.

SERVICE BUSINESSES

Permanent Beauty Care (a beauty shop chain that offers permanents for senior women with thinning hair) targets 165 sites in Virginia, Maryland, and New Jersey with four or more senior apartment complexes within a half-mile radius of the site.

Outsource Computing Power (a firm that runs high-end enterprise resource planning [ERP], customer service, and accounting software for its customers) targets the 285 manufacturers in Southern Illinois, Missouri, and Kansas with sales of $15 to $65 million that use business system software that is over four years old.

PRODUCT-BASED BUSINESSES

Builder Bob (a manufacturer of play tables for children two to seven) targets the over-20,000 child-care centers in the eastern United States that serve over 30 under-five-year-old children per day.

Wall Concepts (a manufacturer of faux painting sponges) targets the 1,500 paint and home improvement stores that sell faux painting glazing paint to do-it-yourself homeowners.

INTERNET BUSINESSES

Raphael's Medical (offers medical information in Spanish plus an extensive list of providers with a staff member(s) who speaks Spanish) targets over 800 medical-related providers in Northern Illinois, Northern Indiana, and Southeastern Wisconsin that target Hispanic consumers.

Investology (provides daily analysis of small capitalization stocks not covered by major firms) targets 95 small to mid-size mutual funds that tout their holdings in small capitalization stocks as an advantage over bigger mutual funds.

Second Goal: Show Importance and Spending Patterns

Clearly defined customers are not enough to make a successful business. The business needs a service that those customers feel is important and that they are willing to purchase at least once, hopefully regularly. Be careful not to overemphasize the resources of your target customers. The important issue is how customers spend their money, not how much they have. Showing importance and spending should be the second phrase in the opening statement. The second phrases below are for the same businesses listed earlier under "First Goal: Define the Customer Group."

LOCAL BUSINESSES

Denny's Auto Repair. The 800 residents spend an average of $625 per year repairing their cars. (Note: the importance of some products and services to the customer is obvious and it is not necessary to state it in the plan.)

Gabrielle's Gifts. Mall statistics show 18% of the targeted daily male visitors, over half from local businesses, spend more than $25 on high-end gifts for wives, girlfriends, or significant others.

DISTRIBUTION BUSINESSES

Advantage Marketing Specialties. 85% of the business-only market expenses are for Yellow Pages ads and promotional items and the firms spend an average of $750 per year on magnets, labels, and other advertising specialties.

Innovative Tooling. Small custom machine shops require

specialized tools for anywhere from one to 10 jobs per year and spend between $750 and $4,000 per tool.

SERVICE BUSINESSES

Permanent Beauty Care. Senior women average one permanent every two months, with a typical permanent costing $75.00.

Outsource Computing Power. These manufacturers are often under pressure from bigger customers to upgrade software to provide increased service, typically have two or three people running the older software, and receive only 50% of the performance of newer software.

PRODUCT-BASED BUSINESSES

Builder Bob. Builder Bob's surveys at two child-care trade shows found that over 60% of child-care centers were searching for toys that encouraged children's creativity and could occupy their attention for over one hour. Established child-care centers spend $2,000 to $15,000 on new play equipment per year and new centers spend between $10,000 and $25,000.

Wall Concepts. Faux painting is now offered by over 50% of professional painters and its use by homeowners has increased 200% per year for the last three years. Over 70% of home and paint stores now feature faux painting supplies.

INTERNET BUSINESSES

Raphael's Medical. A survey of 40 medical providers found that they depended solely on word-of-mouth advertising and were willing to spend $500 per year to increase their Hispanic business.

Investology. Small to mid-size funds can't afford to do their own analysis and are willing to spend $2,000 to $5,000 per year to track five to 10 small-cap stocks that interest them.

Third Goal: Add Emphasis Appropriate for the Business Strategy

Each of the seven business strategies from Chapter 1 requires a slightly different focus regarding customers. For a market maker, the plan wants to show that the customer need is dramatic, while for a market enabler, the crucial point is that the overall market is growing fast.

MARKET MAKER

Key emphasis point: customers have a strong need or desire for the product, service, or store.

Permanent Beauty Care. (It exclusively offers hair care for senior women.) Senior women are not well served by the young stylists of salon chains and want to return to an environment similar to the old neighborhood salon.

MARKET ENABLER

Key emphasis point: the market is growing rapidly.

Wall Concepts. (Its products help neophytes achieve a professional faux painting look in their homes.) Wall Concepts sponges open up faux painting to inexperienced painters to help the market continue its rapid expansion.

TECHNOLOGY LEADER

Key emphasis point: the technology targets a need important to customers.

Outsource Computing Power. (It allows customers to utilize leading-edge, expensive software normally purchased only by large corporations.) Small to mid-size manufacturers understand the benefits of the new software, but they don't have the funds to purchase the software or the staff to execute the conversion.

NICHE MARKETER

Key emphasis point: the customer group is large and stable.

Denny's Auto Repair. (It markets to a limited geographic area.) The Conshohocken area is growing at 4% per year and the demand for auto service should match that growth.

CUSTOMER SOLUTION

Key emphasis point: either customers don't have a current solution or the solution is inadequate.

Innovative Tooling. (It helps small machine shops find custom tools to cost-effectively produce their jobs.) Customers will be able to come to just one source for custom tooling rather than search for the right tool from the over-100 custom tool manufacturers throughout the United States.

PERFORMANCE ENHANCER

Key emphasis point: customers feel that current products, services, or stores don't meet their needs.

Investology. (It offers improved information on certain small-capitalization stocks.) Small to mid-size mutual funds have difficulty offering a unique portfolio of stocks without ongoing company information on small capitalization stocks.

EFFICIENCY IMPROVER

Key emphasis point: the customer need for the product or service is constant or growing.

Advantage Marketing Specialties. (It provides lower costs for promotional magnets and labels by specializing in only those products.) Service businesses' requirements for leave-behind promotional items will increase as the population and the number of service businesses increase.

Conclusion: Restate That a Large Customer Group Needs the Product or Service

The conclusion starts by reemphasizing that you have a size-able customer group with a need for your product, service, or store and that your company can effectively address that need.

LOCAL BUSINESSES

Denny's Auto Repair. The growing community of Conshohocken currently doesn't have a service garage and residents are forced to drive eight miles for service. Denny's Auto Repair will not only be closer, but will also have the community ties that Conshohocken residents prefer for their service businesses.

Gabrielle's Gifts. Gabrielle's primary focus is helping men purchase romantic gifts for the loves of their lives. The large target group of men from surrounding office buildings and homes should match national surveys that show men don't know what gifts to buy, a problem they won't have when they visit Gabrielle's.

DISTRIBUTION BUSINESSES

Advantage Marketing Specialties. The 450 local service businesses in Knoxville rely on people calling them when they need service, but those businesses have trouble keeping their name in front of customers. An effective staple of service business marketing has been promotional giveaways. Advantage Marketing's cost-effective solutions allows businesses to continue with that tradition while cutting their marketing dollars.

Innovative Tooling. Custom machine shops sales are growing, as manufacturers are outsourcing routine production overseas and sending special jobs to the custom shops. Often these jobs are complex and require tools the shops don't have on site. Instead of spending days or hours searching for the part itself, the shops can utilize Innovative Tooling resources to quickly order the right tool.

SERVICE BUSINESSES

Permanent Beauty Care. The rapid rise in seniors moving to apartments has taken senior women away from their neighborhood hair stylists and left them searching for salons that can do permanents that add body to their thinning hair. Salon chains like Cost Cutters and Great Clips focus on younger customers, leaving senior customers to search for a better solution for their needs, a solution Permanent Beauty Care provides.

Outsource Computing Power. Small to mid-size companies' major customers are demanding just-in-time delivery, lean manufacturing practices, and support for Six Sigma quality programs. Target customers can't meet those increasing requirements on their own without software upgrades. Outsource Computing Power software services let them offer state-of-the-art manufacturing practices to support their customers.

PRODUCT-BASED BUSINESSES

Builder Bob. Child-care centers throughout the country that focus on mid- to upper-income families are increasingly being asked to provide interactive play time that fosters creativity. Builder Bob products are designed by three early childhood education teachers and are approved by the National Association for the Education of Young Children. Builder Bob products provide an excellent tool for its customers to market their services to parents with children.

Wall Concepts. Home centers succeed by offering products and services for all of the home improvement needs of do-it-yourself homeowners. Faux painting is now a hot new trend and Wall Concepts Print Sponges allow paint and home centers to provide a cutting-edge product line for both experienced and first-time faux painters.

INTERNET BUSINESSES

Raphael's Medical. 10% to 15% of the medical centers in Chicago are anxious to reach Hispanics, the fastest-growing population in the greater Chicago area. Raphael's Medical web site, with key ties to Hispanic area community centers and service groups, provides a fast, easy marketing tool for Raphael's to reach target customers in the Hispanic community.

Investology. Over 50% of small to mid-size mutual funds promote their ability to follow small-capitalization stocks as a benefit to potential buyers. Small-capitalization stocks offer potential for major stock gains, but only if the funds can keep current with each company's status through the use of independent research, a key service where Investology leads the market.

Chapter 12
Market Drivers:
The Building Blocks of Success

Market drivers are the underlying reason that a market should thrive; they are referred to throughout a plan, as they contribute strongly to a business' success. The most important aspect of a market driver is that it implies market growth, which is a strong predictor of business success. Companies can't dictate what the drivers are, but they can orient their businesses to capitalize on them. Businesses in markets with strong drivers have greater room for error, greater possibilities for growth, and the ability to generate significantly higher profits. The businesses discussed in Chapter 3 include many market drivers, including the following:

- **Outsource Computing Power:** Large customers are demanding improved efficiency from their vendors.
- **Builder Bob:** Parents increasingly want child-care centers to provide enrichment opportunities for their children.
- **Permanent Beauty Care:** Senior apartment complexes, with provisions for assisted living, are rapidly being built in every section of the country.

Power Paragraph

Elements of the Power Paragraph

- **First goal:** Identify the market drivers.
- **Second goal:** Show impact on customers.
- **Third goal:** Add emphasis appropriate for the business strategy.
- **Conclusion:** Restate that the company can capitalize on the opportunity.

Sample Power Paragraph

This power paragraph is for the AutoV Editor. (See Chapter 3, page 18 for the company description.)

Digital video is available now in camcorders, digital cameras, and camera phones. People have access to video today as never before. *[First goal: identify the market drivers.]* The AutoV Editor's target customers, manufacturers of digital video equipment, are capitalizing on the market with new products and rapidly expanding sales. *[Second goal: show impact on customers.]* The AutoV Editor easy-to-use features are based on patented software that is faster and requires fewer steps than competing software products. *[Third goal: add emphasis appropriate for the business strategy: a new competitor won't quickly erase the company's performance advantage.]* The AutoV Editor is ready for the market, it has passed extensive consumer tests, and the company has contract negotiations under way at three major digital video equipment suppliers. *[Conclusion: restate that the company can capitalize on the opportunity.]*

Applicable Plan Sections

You should consider adding elements of the market driver power paragraph to these sections of the business plan.

1b. Executive Summary—Business Concept or Description

1d. Executive Summary—Target Market and Market Drivers

3a. Target Markets—Market Drivers

5a. Key Advantage—Customers' Priorities

7d. Marketing Strategy—Alliances

First Goal: Identify the Market Drivers

Market drivers are normally created by a shift in the market, which can be caused by many factors.

*1. **Regulation:*** *New emission standards set by the EPA for trucks and cars create huge market drivers for emission control products.*

*2. **Technology:*** *The Internet created market drivers in or for telecommunications hardware, Internet service providers (ISPs), consumer and business software, computer hardware, and high-speed Internet connection devices.*

*3. **Lifestyle changes:*** *People with more leisure time, more disposable income, increased interest in cooking and exercise, or increased use of child-care services all create drivers for growth in related markets.*

*4. **Customer demands:*** *Businesses might want one-week delivery from vendors, parents might want more enrichment opportunities for their children, and restaurant users might want to have more entertainment with their meals.*

*5. **Related market developments:*** *The popularity of senior apartments with options for assisted living creates market drivers for related services, including transportation, Internet grocery services, video rental, and delivery of prescription medicines.*

*6. **Population growth:*** *New neighborhoods create market drivers for all types of businesses needed to support the needs of those neighborhoods.*

*7. **Business practices:*** *Electronic data exchange required by big retailers is a market driver for electronic data services and software for small companies.*

LOCAL BUSINESSES

Denny's Auto Repair (four-bay auto repair garage). Conshohocken residents want to do business with local merchants.

Gabrielle's Gifts (high-end gift shop for women). Men increasingly want to give romantic gifts to their significant others.

DISTRIBUTION BUSINESSES

Advantage Marketing Specialties (advertising promotion specialties). Increasing population and competition in Knoxville require service companies to increase marketing efforts.

Innovative Tooling (coordinates with an alliance of custom tool manufacturers to provide any required custom tool). Large manufacturers today source machining projects only to American shops that can find ways to machine difficult custom projects.

SERVICE BUSINESS

Permanent Beauty Care (a beauty shop chain that offers permanents for senior women with thinning hair). The building boom in senior housing has concentrated senior women like never before.

Outsource Computing Power (a firm that runs high-end enterprise resource planning [ERP], customer service, and accounting software for its customers). Big companies are demanding that vendors' software interface with their advanced software for improved productivity.

PRODUCT-BASED BUSINESSES

Builder Bob (a manufacturer of play tables for children two to seven). Mid- and high-income parents are demanding that child-care centers increase their enrichment activities.

Wall Concepts (a manufacturer of faux painting sponges). Faux painting has become a popular decorating scheme for homeowners, who are either hiring decorators and professional painters or starting to do faux painting on their own.

INTERNET BUSINESS

Raphael's Medical (offers medical information in Spanish and an extensive list of providers with a staff member(s) who speaks Spanish). The number of Hispanics in the Greater Chicago area is increasing by over 15% per year.

Investology (provides daily analysis of small-capitalization stocks). Investors are increasingly looking to invest in small to mid-size mutual funds with unique investment strategies to obtain the highest yields.

Second Goal: Show Impact on Customers

A market driver forces action from the company's target customer. The next perfect phrase has to express the action customers take in response to that driver. In some cases the company's target customers might take several actions in response to the market driver. For instance, Investology's target customers, small to mid-size mutual funds, might strive for higher returns by investing in foreign markets, purchasing options, or investing in small-capitalization stocks. Investology helps companies with one of those choices, investing in small-capitalization stocks.

LOCAL BUSINESSES

Denny's Auto Repair. 60% of Conshohocken's residents purchase from local service providers whenever possible.

Gabrielle's Gifts. 83% of men surveyed state they have purchased flowers as a romantic gift after searching in vain for a "special" gift for their significant other.

DISTRIBUTION BUSINESSES

Advantage Marketing Specialties. Service businesses that promote their services over and above their Yellow Pages ads report 15% sales increases.

Innovative Tooling. Custom machine shop engineers spend 10 to 20 hours trying to locate tooling and then determine tooling costs prior to bidding a job.

SERVICE BUSINESS

Permanent Beauty Care. A high percentage of elderly women who arrange for transportation back to their former neighborhoods to shop explain that they make the trip because they don't know shops in their new neighborhoods.

Outsource Computing Power. Most small manufacturers are currently responding to the demand for just-in-time delivery by adding inventory and administrative staffing and trying to add patches to their current software.

PRODUCT-BASED BUSINESSES

Builder Bob. In response to parents' search for enrichment activities, child-care centers are adding classes and purchasing educational materials and toys.

Wall Concepts. Over 70% of paint and home centers have added specific sections dedicated to faux painting to serve this rapidly growing market.

INTERNET BUSINESSES

Raphael's Medical. A significant percentage of medical providers have added Spanish-speaking staff and certain providers are starting to offer outreach service in churches and community centers in Hispanic areas.

Investology. The majority of small mutual funds now promote at least one specialized investment strategy that is too small for major funds, creating opportunities for potentially higher yields.

Third Goal: Add Emphasis Appropriate for the Business Strategy

Each of the seven business strategies from Chapter 1 requires a slightly different focus regarding market drivers. For a market maker, the plan should show that the driver is recent and that the company is on the cutting edge of a new opportunity. For a technology leader, the crucial point is that the technological challenges of introducing the new technology have been conquered and that the risk of introducing the product or service is low.

MARKET MAKER

Key emphasis point: the market driver is recent. Readers will wonder why no one else has capitalized on the opportunity if it has existed for some time.

Permanent Beauty Care. While senior complexes have been increasing rapidly for the last five years, only recently has the growth led to clusters of four to five complexes within a half-mile radius to justify the transportation that Permanent Beauty Care provides.

MARKET ENABLER

Key emphasis point: the market is recognized and proven.

Wall Concepts. The faux painting market has recently been recognized by several trade journals and has been featured at several trade shows and there are now seven suppliers of faux painting glazing paints. The Sponge Prince will be a key part of this market expanding even faster as it will help more novices try faux painting.

TECHNOLOGY LEADER
Key emphasis point: the risk of introducing the new technology is minimal.

Outsource Computing Power. Outsource Computing Power offers manufacturers the best technology available, with few if any start-up problems as the software has been tested and proved at large companies for the last three years.

NICHE MARKETER
Key emphasis point: the market is unlikely to change.

Denny's Auto Repair. Conshohocken is a blue-collar town that depends on a prospering Owens Corning plant. While the neighborhood has grown with increases in plant employment, most residents have lived in Conshohocken over 10 years.

CUSTOMER SOLUTION
Key emphasis point: either that the market is large and can support many solution providers or that the market is unlikely to attract additional competition.

Innovative Tooling. Innovative Tooling has targeted Texas and Oklahoma manufacturers because the market, while large, is distant from the major machine shop markets of the East Coast and California so that the company can form strong relationships with its customers.

PERFORMANCE ENHANCER
Key emphasis point: a new competitor won't quickly erase the company's performance advantage.

Investology. Mutual fund customers are skeptical of a new firm's trend analysis and Investology expects to hold onto and expand its customer base as long as it provides quality information.

EFFICIENCY IMPROVER

Key emphasis point: customers in the market already purchase the product(s) or service(s) and they will recognize and value the improved efficiency and costs.

Advantage Marketing Specialties. Service businesses currently are purchasing in-home marketing materials from Atlanta or mail order catalogs. Advantage Marketing Specialties will be able to work with Knoxville companies to produce the products they want while still cutting their costs.

Conclusion: Restate That the Company Can Capitalize on the Opportunity

Market drivers are created by shifts in the market that create opportunities for companies to provide products and services that better meet customers' new needs and desires. The conclusion needs to be clear that the company is in a strong position to capitalize on a new opportunity in the market.

LOCAL BUSINESSES

Denny's Auto Service. Conshohocken residents strongly patronize available local businesses but have been forced to drive eight miles to Norristown for service. Denny's Auto Service will fill the key void for auto service in this growing community.

Gabrielle's Gifts. The market opportunity in helping men buy romantic gifts is huge, as men don't like shopping and don't know what to buy to show their romantic side. Gabrielle's Gifts fills a void with $25 to $400 presents that will satisfy the most demanding significant other.

DISTRIBUTION BUSINESS

Advantage Marketing Specialties. Knoxville area businesses know they need to increase their marketing efforts but the lack of a local provider that understands their needs often results in companies choosing the wrong solution. Advantage Marketing Specialties' local presence will fill this void and help its customers cost-effectively improve their marketing efforts.

Innovative Tooling. Custom machine shops have seen a

20% increase in bid requests as major companies cut back on their own machining centers. Most of these bids are for highly specialized machining operations and many times the companies don't bid because they can't locate the proper tooling to bid on the job. Innovative Tooling will help its customers bid and win more jobs.

SERVICE BUSINESSES

Permanent Beauty Care. The proliferation of senior citizen housing in certain suburban areas provides a ready base of senior women looking for the type of permanents that hide their thinning hair. Permanent Beauty Care has the right equipment and stylists to serve this market and should be able to achieve 25% market share by offering transportation services.

Outsource Computing Power. Most small to mid-size companies don't have the software or the funds to buy it to effectively meet the shipment requirements of their customers. Outsource Computing Power cost-effectively offers the computing capabilities that small to mid-size manufacturers need to meet their customers' demands.

PRODUCT-BASED BUSINESSES

Builder Bob. Child-care centers, historically on tight equipment budgets, are looking for low-cost purchases to satisfy parents looking for more enrichment for their children. Builder Bob's products are an ideal solution, not only because of their modest costs but because its type of product is established as a toy that fosters creativity.

Wall Concepts. Paint and home center stores generate significant profits from high-margin faux painting items. They are looking for new products to expand the market to more homeowners and Wall Concepts' Print Sponges are an ideal product for the novice faux painter. Wall Concepts expects that at least 50% of stores with faux painting centers will add the Sponge Prince line.

INTERNET BUSINESSES

Raphael's Medical. Many new Hispanic residents have not yet chosen their health-care providers and it is a customer group many medical providers want to reach. Ralphael's Medical offers a low-cost information source that can be offered through Internet access computers at Hispanic churches and community centers to help those providers establish a Hispanic customer base.

Investology. Small to mid-size mutual funds are struggling to add clients in today's tough market conditions. Their major response to these conditions is to search for ways to offer potentially higher yields. One tactic firms are using is a willingness to hold small-capitalization stocks. Investology analysis of those stocks opens up marketing opportunities for its customers, allowing them to compete with the larger, more established mutual funds.

Chapter 13
Market Size: Offer Plenty of Room for Growth

Market is a term to describe the buying and selling activity of a type of product. For example, the market for Magnolene's Restaurant is the upscale restaurant market in the western suburbs of Nashville, Tennessee. The market includes the customers, people who eat at upscale restaurants, and the businesses that serve those customers. The goal of most plans is to show that the company participates in a market with a rapidly expanding customer base.

Power Paragraph

Elements of the Power Paragraph

- **First goal:** Describe the market and indicate its size.
- **Second goal:** Explain why the market is growing.
- **Third goal:** Add emphasis appropriate for the business strategy.
- **Conclusion:** The company is relevant to why the market is growing.

Sample Power Paragraph

This power paragraph is for a DepositCash ATM card, which is targeted at wage earners who don't keep bank accounts. A customer can have his or her paychecks deposited directly into his or her DepositCash ATM card and then access the money at any ATM as well as using the card as a debit card anywhere that Visa cards are accepted. The card eliminates the expense of high check-cashing fees.

DepositCash ATM Card participates in the $25-billion-per-year payroll-check-cashing market. *[First goal: describe the market and indicate its size.]* Currently 25 million wage earners do not have bank accounts, primarily new and illegal immigrants, whose numbers are increasing every year. *[Second goal: explain why the market is growing.]* DepositCash ATM card allows employers to direct-deposit paychecks and saves users a 3% to 5% check-cashing charge. *[Third goal: add emphasis appropriate for the business strategy. DepositCash is a market maker; the emphasis is that current products on the market are inadequate.]* DepositCash's services, which include Western Union-type money transfers, are geared to immigrants and DepositCash has placed its offices in neighborhoods with significant immigrant population. *[Conclusion: the company is relevant to why the market is growing.]*

Applicable Plan Sections

1e. Executive Summary—Market Size and Niche

3a. Target Markets—Market Drivers

7b. Marketing Strategy—Pricing and Gross Margins

First Goal: Describe the Market and Indicate Its Size

You have two choices when describing the market. You can choose only the market with products you compete against directly, referred to as the narrow market, or you can list the market that includes products or services people buy for the same purpose, referred to as a broad market. For example, DepositCash could list its market as direct-deposit accounts for people without bank accounts, or it could list a broader market, check cashing, which would include check-cashing businesses and pawn shops. Since DepositCash is a market maker, there is no market for its product. Check-cashing businesses serve the same target customer, so it is reasonable to include check cashing as part of the same market. I've noted in the examples if the market described is broad or narrow to help you see the distinctions between the two types of market.

LOCAL BUSINESSES

Johnson Dental (three dentists and two hygienists serving new housing developments) provides dental service to the new Briarwood and Oakwood developments (narrow). The total of dental work in similar-size developments in Oklahoma City averages $3 million.

Guitar World (retail store with new and used guitars and accessories) is in Knoxville, Tennessee, where guitar and accessory sales (broad) in general music stores or through catalogs or Internet sales, are estimated at $6 to $7 million per year.

DISTRIBUTION BUSINESSES

ABC Roofing (distributor of roofing supplies to 85 roofing companies) focuses on the $700-million market for distinctive roofing materials in Virginia, Georgia, Tennessee, and North and South Carolina (broad).

Gannet Sales (supplying and servicing a complete line of soft-serve frozen yogurt and smoothie equipment) services the $8-million Arizona, New Mexico, and Utah market for soft-serve frozen yogurt and smoothie equipment (narrow).

SERVICE BUSINESSES

City Course Catering (exclusive rights to staging events, primarily weddings and rehearsal dinners, in two 1920s-era golf course clubhouses) is in the market of wedding, rehearsal, and large dinner events for over 100 people in Minneapolis (broad). The 1,800 to 2,000 events per year generate approximately $20 million per year in revenue.

Closed Caption Theatre Technology (CCTT) (providing closed-captioning equipment to theaters for a monthly fee) has as its target markets theaters from Massachusetts to Virginia under pressure from advocates for the hearing-impaired to add closed-captioning capability (narrow). The current market size for monthly rentals is approximately $25,000 per month, or $300,000 per year.

PRODUCT-BASED BUSINESSES

Club Runner (manufacturer of a battery-operated motorized golf pull cart) competes in the $14-million U.S. motorized walking golf cart market, both for clubs that rent motorized carts and consumers who own carts (narrow).

MediaTile Smart Signs (signs with wireless connectivity for retail stores, enabling stores to change in-store signs from the office) serves the electronic in-store supermarket sign market (broad), a $185-million-per-year market in the United States.

INTERNET BUSINESSES

BankIntelligence (providing current money market rates, national loan rates, and federal fund rates to banks and investment firms) is in the market of selling rate and fund data and related information to banks and other financial institutions (broad), an $8-million-per-year market.

PokerMania.com (site with poker instruction, supplies, accessories, and news on upcoming tournaments by state) competes in the poker information market, which includes Internet sites, newsletters, and magazines (broad), a $7.5-million market nationally.

Second Goal: Explain Why the Market Is Growing

Businesses have the most success in growing markets, where there is sufficient business for all competitors. Most fast-growth businesses with high margins compete in rapidly growing markets.

LOCAL BUSINESSES

Johnson Dental. The new Briarwood and Oakwood developments are growing at a rate of 15% per year.

Guitar World. An increasing percentage of teenage boys are taking up the guitar and the market's 18% growth rate is fueled about 50/50 by new users and higher-cost equipment.

DISTRIBUTION BUSINESSES

ABC Roofing. The market for distinctive shingles is increasing at 12% per year, mirroring the market growth for custom homes and high-end developments.

Gannet Sales. The market for smoothie and soft-serve yogurt equipment is increasing over 20% per year as those two product categories are being picked up as dessert items at coffeehouses.

SERVICE BUSINESSES

City Course Catering. The event-dinner market size is increasing 6% per year, fueled primarily by the upgraded food menus and the increase in availability of more upscale event settings.

Closed Caption Theatre Technology. Closed captioning for theaters is growing over 200% per year, since the technology is new and advocate groups are just starting to pressure theaters into adding closed captioning for the hearing-impaired.

PRODUCT-BASED BUSINESSES

Club Runner. The market for motorized walking carts is increasing 20% per year, as the popularity of the carts with women and seniors has spread nationwide from its initial regional pocket markets.

MediaTile Smart Signs. The in-store electronic supermarket sign market is increasing 15% per year as more and more stores are changing over from their printed signage systems.

INTERNET BUSINESSES

BankIntelligence. The bank information market grows 6% to 10% per year as banks strive to compete in a market where consumers have the ability to compare prices, rates, and fees over the Internet.

PokerMania.com. Poker tournaments carried live on cable TV and local card rooms have created widespread interest in poker. People who play poker at clubs or at home have increased by over five million in the last 12 months alone.

Third Goal: Add Emphasis Appropriate for the Business Strategy

Each of the seven business strategies from Chapter 1 requires a slightly different focus regarding markets. For a market enabler, the plan should show that market growth is driven by new customers, new applications, and old customers that need additional services or features, creating a new opportunity. A niche marketer wants to explain that the market will continue to grow.

MARKET MAKER

Key emphasis point: current products on the market are inadequate.

MediaTile Smart Signs. Current electronic sign systems require reprogramming for each sign, a time-consuming process that is more expensive than printed signs. MediaTile Smart Signs, with wireless connections, can be quickly reprogrammed from the store's office.

MARKET ENABLER

Key emphasis point: new customers or new applications are fueling the market's growth.

PokerMania.com. National, TV, and local poker tournaments are creating enormous interest in poker for people who previously have not participated. New players, not wanting to lose money, are devouring information on strategy and buying products to play with their friends before entering a casino or club tournaments.

TECHNOLOGY LEADER

Key emphasis point: the new technology offers significant benefits to users.

Closed Captioning Theatre Technology. CCTT's technology is localized at the user's seat, so the other members of the audience are not distracted by on-screen closed captioning.

NICHE MARKETER

Key emphasis point: the market growth is likely to continue.

Guitar World. The market for guitar equipment, especially for larger amplifiers, continues to grow with expanding opportunities for bands to perform in under-21 shows and clubs across the country.

CUSTOMER SOLUTION

Key emphasis point: having a complete solution is important to the market.

Gannet Sales. The coffee stores want the income from dessert-oriented items, but only if it is trouble-free. Otherwise they will just continue to offer cheesecakes, pies, and pastries available from local bakeries.

PERFORMANCE ENHANCER

Key emphasis point: customers value the increased performance.

Club Runner. Motorized walking carts allow golfers who prefer walking to continue to do so even if they are unable or unwilling to use a pull golf cart. The product has been very successful at clubs with a large number of seniors and women, who feel the product is more than worth its $650 price.

EFFICIENCY IMPROVER

Key emphasis point: increased efficiency is a value to the market.

ABC Roofing. ABC's ability to offer quick delivery on over 256 types of roofing products provides a big advantage over Home Depot, which offers 10 to 15 varieties of shingles and smaller distrributors, which offer 30 to 50 types of shingles.

Conclusion: The Company Is Relevant to Why the Market Is Growing

LOCAL BUSINESSES

Johnson Dental. New families with young children are moving into the developments, and the Johnson Dental practice and office focuses on the needs of young families, with special pediatric services including sealants, orthodontic services, and a room with equipment specifically designed for young children, in order to capture a major share of the business from the growing market.

Guitar World. In addition to performance-oriented guitars and amplifiers, Guitar World includes a sound stage and recording studio, available for hourly rental, postings for performance opportunities, and a bulletin board for band openings to capitalize on the performance aspects of the market's growth.

DISTRIBUTION BUSINESSES

ABC Roofing. ABC's large variety of inventory perfectly positions the company to capitalize on builders' and homeowners' desire for a distinctive look to their homes.

Gannet Sales. Trouble-free performance for smoothie and soft yogurt equipment supports the rapid growth of the after-dinner coffeehouse market as it allows owners to concentrate on ambience and entertainment, rather than how their equipment is operating.

SERVICE BUSINESSES

City Course Catering. City Course Catering offers its services in 1920s historic golf course clubhouses with big romantic ballrooms with some of the best and most distinctive ambience in the area and offers excellent venues for the increasingly upscale events in the Twin Cities.

Closed Caption Theatre Technology. CCTT offers theater owners a low-upfront-cost option to help theaters meet demands for full movie access to the hearing-impaired without impacting other audience members. CCTT is positioned to take a market share of 75% or more in this market as it rapidly develops.

PRODUCT-BASED BUSINESSES

Club Runner. Club Runner has expanded its distribution to include golf catalogs, pro shops at golf courses, and off-site golf retailers such as Nevada Bob's so the product is available to senior golfers no matter where they shop or play, in order to expand the product's use throughout the country.

MediaTile Smart Signs. The electronic in-store supermarket sign market is growing because of its instant-change capabilities, a capability that is greatly enhanced with MediaTile's wireless capability. MediaTile expects the electronic sign market to grow even faster with the quicker changes and lower labor requirements of wireless products.

INTERNET BUSINESSES

BankIntelligence. Banks constantly search for instant information to keep competitive, and BankIntelligence's Advisory Board from 12 banks provides steady flow of new information for their needs, which not only adds to BankIntelligence's service portfolio, but also increases the rate of the market's growth.

PokerMania.com. The poker PokerMania Web site targets the market growth in new players by placing a strong emphasis on its PokerU feature for new players and offering input into clubs and casinos where lower-limit games are played.

Chapter 14
Market Niche: A Space
That Produces Profits

The last three chapters helped you establish that you have an impressive opportunity: good customers, strong market drivers, and a growing market. Once you establish that the product will sell into a robust market environment, the next step is to establish that you have a good competitive position in that market.

The next three chapters on market niche, competitive advantage, and proprietary advantages all deal with how the company will position itself as a leader in the market. After all, your company won't be the only one observing that an ideal market opportunity is emerging. The market niche chapter will help you demonstrate that you have found a specific market where your advantage is most important, the competitive advantage is how your company will stand out against competitors, and the proprietary chapter deals with how you can prevent or delay competitors from copying your business strategy.

Market niche is the specific market arena or circumstances in which a business sells its products or services. For example, the market niche for a playground equipment manufacturer might be church-based day-care centers sold through manufacturers' representatives, catalogs, and a Web site. Other market niches for playground equipment include homeowners, schools, secular day-care centers, parks, and large commercial markets like McDonald's. Only the largest companies typically have the resources to compete in all market niches. Companies usually succeed by allocating their resources to one or two market niches.

Power Paragraph

Elements of the Power Paragraph

- **First goal:** Describe the market niche.
- **Second goal:** Explain why your product or service is a good fit for that niche.
- **Third goal:** Add emphasis appropriate for the business strategy.
- **Conclusion:** The company has chosen a market in which it can successfully compete.

Sample Power Paragraph

This power paragraph is for Schuylkill Valley Medical, which offers emergency medical training to employees of major U.S. corporations, with training that lasts from one to four weeks in addition to a three-day CPR-only training. In its business plan, Schuylkill Valley Medical is trying to raise $500,000 to increase its staff from three

> Schuylkill Valley's market niche is emergency medical training for staff at mid-size to large corporations in the mid-Atlantic region. *[First goal: describe the market niche.]* Schuylkill Valley's three-week course offers training for personnel who can take

---

emergency action until medical help arrives, a convenient option for companies as an alternative to a two-year course for paramedics. *[Second goal: explain why your product or service is a good fit for that niche; and Third goal: add emphasis appropriate for the business strategy. Schuylkill Valley is a performance enhancer; its emphasis is that current products don't serve the market adequately.]* In Schuylkill Valley's first two years of operation, over 90 corporations have inquired about training. With increased staff, Schuylkill Valley will be able to certify class participants, a key requirement for corporate training. *[Conclusion: the company has chosen a market in which it can successfully compete.]*

---

to eight people and to expand its training facility.

Applicable Plan Sections

1e. Executive Summary—Market Size and Niche
3d. Target Market—Market Niche

First Goal: Describe the Market Niche

Your market niche should be very specific, describing only your key initial target market, where your marketing efforts will be focused. Schuylkill Valley's training, for instance, could be for corporations throughout the country, but it is marketing only to companies in the mid-Atlantic region, so in the plan it restricts the market niche to that specific area. Your market niche might expand in later years, but the plan should list only the area to which you will market in the next two years.

LOCAL BUSINESSES

Rudy's RV Center (a large Denver, Colorado, RV dealer). Rudy's RV Center's market niche is the geographic area within 250 miles of Denver.

ZZ's Organic Restaurant (organically grown fruits and vegetables and pasture-raised, hormone- and antibiotic-free meat). ZZ's Organic Restaurant's market niche is health-conscious 20- to 35-year-olds in the resurging neighborhood west of downtown Atlanta.

DISTRIBUTION BUSINESSES

Esthetics Plus (full-service supplier of skin care products). Esthetics Plus's market niche is spas and salons in California and Arizona that employ professional estheticians.

Little Rock Candy (supplier of bulk candy to supermarkets). Little Rock Candy's market niche is regional supermarkets in the rural areas of Arkansas, Mississippi, and Louisiana.

SERVICE BUSINESSES

Anesthesiology Billing (billing and insurance claims service). Anesthesiology Billing's market niche is hospital-based anesthesiology practices east of the Mississippi River.

Mubix2buzz (instant messaging service over smart phones and PDAs. When customers want to do a multiple-party call, they send Mubix2buzz [via phone or PDA] a contact list. Mubix2buzz then sends a message to each contact with a number to call to be a part of the multiparty call.) Mubix2buzz's target market niche is under-25-year-olds in Boston, Massachusetts, Providence, Rhode Island, and Hartford, Connecticut.

PRODUCT-BASED BUSINESSES

LWO2 (supplier of oxygen cylinders for medical use at one-fourth the weight of traditional oxygen cylinders). LWO2's market niche is fire companies, ambulance services, and nursing homes in Illinois, Michigan, Indiana, and Pennsylvania.

Jetboil Personal Cooking System (outdoors complete cooking system, with cooking vessel, flame, and fuel source contained in a patented flux ring for fast and safe cooking in any conditions). Jetboil Personal Cooking System's initial market includes backpacking catalogs and outdoor stores like REI and Gander Mountain.

INTERNET BUSINESSES

Virtual Due Diligence (electronic storage of all documents pertinent to any business deal, but especially mergers and acquisitions, with a site that enables all parties to access data simultaneously, rather than each party in succession). Virtual Due Diligence's market niche is investment bankers and legal firms associated with mergers and acquisitions.

Swapalease.com (a site that allows a person leasing an auto to find someone to take over that auto lease). Swapalease.com's market niche is people wanting to assume or exit an auto lease with more than two years left on its term.

Second Goal: Explain Why Your Product or Service Is a Good Fit for That Niche

The whole idea behind a market niche is that you have chosen a market you can afford to attack and that you have created the perfect product for the market segment. Ideally your plan or service will have specific benefits that your market wants. Schuylkill Valley Medical offers the specific emergency medical training corporations want, training that takes less time but is still good enough to offer emergency support prior to the arrival of the medical team. Businesses have a strong chance of success when they have the right product or service for the market.

LOCAL BUSINESSES

Rudy's RV Center. Colorado RV customers are often pragmatic ranchers who shop carefully. Rudy's RV Center, by far the largest RV dealer in the area, is large enough to have nine factory representatives on site, providing the detailed product information Rudy's customers want.

ZZ's Organic Restaurant. ZZ's Organic Restaurant target neighborhood is primarily young urban professionals who already support two organic grocery store co-ops in the area. ZZ's, specializing in organic food, special meals, and low-fat cooking, appeals to the co-op's customer base.

DISTRIBUTION BUSINESSES

Esthetics Plus. Besides offering a full line of professional skin care products to estheticians, Esthetics Plus offers a newsletter and Web site with the latest information to keep estheticians one step ahead of their trend-setting customers.

Little Rock Candy. The major supermarket distributors have started to ignore rural supermarkets; Little Rock Candy's small size and personal service are a good fit for rural supermarkets.

SERVICE BUSINESSES

Anesthesiology Billing. Anesthesiologist insurance claims are significantly different from standard medical claims and, if they are done incorrectly, insurance companies reject them or pay less than the minimum. Anesthesiology Billing's specialization offers its customers fast turnaround and reimbursement.

Mubix2buzz. Teens and young adults want always-on conference capability to talk with their friends about what they are doing that evening or even that moment. Mubix2buzz takes teens and adults with cell phones one step further, to the instant group conversation.

PRODUCT-BASED BUSINESSES

LWO2. Traditional oxygen cylinders are heavy and hard for fire and medical users to maneuver. A lightweight cylinder is more maneuverable and can be put in use in half the time of a traditional cylinder, a key factor for users trying to save lives.

Jetboil Personal Cooking System. The Jetboil system is ideal for bad weather, when backpackers traditionally must survive without hot food, and is lightweight and easy to pack, all key benefits to mountain hikers.

INTERNET BUSINESSES

Virtual Due Diligence. Shifting documents back and forth takes time and it keeps investment bankers and lawyers from having access to all the documents they might need. Virtual Due Diligence's data rooms cut the typical time for due diligence in half.

Swapalease.com. Auto leases historically have taken away people's freedom to exit a car lease either to get another car or to get rid of a financial obligation. Swapalease.com removes the chains, offering leaseholders an easy exit strategy and offering buyers a chance to pick up a short-term lease on an older car.

Third Goal: Add Emphasis Appropriate for the Business Strategy

Each of the seven business strategies from Chapter 1 requires a slightly different focus regarding market niche. For example, a company providing a complete solution wants to explain that the solution is perfect for the market niche, while a company that offers increased efficiency wants to explain how efficiency is important to customers.

MARKET MAKER

Key emphasis point: the market niche will be receptive to a new concept.

ZZ's Organic Restaurant. ZZ's Organic Restaurant has located a chef with a strong organic cooking background who wants to move to Atlanta, and the signature meals and upscale atmosphere make it the restaurant that Atlanta organic food lovers, tired of boring meals, have indicated they want.

MARKET ENABLER

Key emphasis point: companies in the market niche have recognized the value of the product or service.

Virtual Due Diligence. Many firms are reluctant to enter a merger or acquisition because of the time-consuming and expensive due diligence process for deals, many of which don't go through. Investment bankers and legal firms use Virtual Due Diligence as a sales tool since it allows a firm to know in 30 days whether or not a deal is possible.

TECHNOLOGY LEADER

Key emphasis point: the new technology will be easy to implement.

Mubix2buzz. The Mubix2buzz equipment supplier has systems up and running in three other markets and Mubix2buzz should be able to introduce its service with a minimum of technical problems.

NICHE MARKETER

Key emphasis point: the company offers a major advantage to the market niche.

Anesthesiology Billing. Anesthesiology Billing acquires 90% of its customers through word-of-mouth advertising since the reimbursement time of general medical billing services averages four months.

CUSTOMER SOLUTION

Key emphasis point: the solution is perfect for the market niche.

Jetboil Personal Cooking System. The Jetboil Personal Cooking System is lightweight and easy to carry and it works in every weather situation, making it a perfect solution for backpackers looking to pack as light as possible yet still enjoy hot food.

PERFORMANCE ENHANCER

Key emphasis point: current products don't serve the market adequately.

LWO2. Speed is critical to fire and emergency medical personnel, and the current large oxygen cylinders are hard to maneuver in a crisis.

EFFICIENCY IMPROVER

Key emphasis point: efficiency is important to customers.

Rudy's RV Center. Rudy's RV Center simplifies the process of buying an RV, allowing customers to see all the major brands at one location and to ask detailed questions of RV manufacturers' representatives.

Conclusion: The Company Has Chosen a Market in Which It Can Successfully Compete

LOCAL BUSINESSES

Rudy's RV Center. Rudy's RV Center has a strong market position because it has the most inventory, all of the major brands, and offers the best source of RV product information in the Denver area.

ZZ's Organic Restaurant. ZZ's Organic Restaurant will be a significant addition in the neighborhood as it offers residents an upscale organic dining experience, capitalizing on the high interest in organic foods generated by local co-op grocers.

DISTRIBUTION BUSINESSES

Esthetics Plus. Esthetics Plus's full-line offering, plus working through both the Web and sales representatives, will allow it to duplicate or come close to the 60% market share the company has in the Washington, DC area, its other targeted markets.

Little Rock Candy. With the acquisition of a competitor, Little Rock Candy will be able to dominate sales to rural supermarkets, offering a line as big as the major city distributors, while supplying a higher level of service to smaller supermarkets.

SERVICE BUSINESSES

Anesthesiology Billing. Anesthesiology Billing has a 70% closing rate on accounts it targets due to its specialized service; its increased technical capability should allow it to expand its success to new markets.

Mubix2buzz. No customer buzz is greater than the buzz created by "hot" products for the teen or young adult market. Mubix2buzz has a product young people want and it expects to convince 10% to 15% of potential customers to sign up within the first 12 months.

PRODUCT-BASED BUSINESSES

Jetboil Personal Cooking System. Jetboil Personal Cooking System has a new PR campaign ready to release when it can increase production; both REI and Gander Mountain have indicated they will carry the product once it has a more "professional," durable appearance.

LWO2. LWO2 has formed an initial relationship with one oxygen distributor that has agreed to offer the new cylinders as another option to the larger cylinders. LWO2's market research indicates over half of the potential oxygen users will request the smaller cylinders and LWO2 expects to add distributors after its initial market success.

INTERNET BUSINESSES

Virtual Due Diligence. Service, not cost, is important to Virtual Due Diligence's customers and the improved technology allows Virtual Due Diligence to offer the fastest retrieval time available in the market.

Swapalease.com. Most auto leaseholders are unaware that they can transfer a lease from one person to another. Swapalease.com has only two small competitors and its increased promotion and awareness, along with better customer information, should propel it to a significant market share over the next 12 months.

Chapter 15
Competitive Advantage:
How You Stand Out

The competitive advantage is how your company will stand out against competitors, the niche market chapter will help you demonstrate that you have found a specific market where your advantage is most important, and the proprietary chapter deals with how you can prevent or delay competitors from copying your business strategy.

A competitive advantage can be in any number of areas. You could have the ideal location, certain product features, as well-known employee, the best solution for certain applications, partnerships with key industry contacts, an exclusive contract with a key vendor, or the best distribution network.

Power Paragraph

Elements of the Power Paragraph

- **First goal:** Describe the advantage.
- **Second goal:** Explain why the advantage is important.
- **Third goal:** Add emphasis appropriate for the business strategy.

■ **Conclusion:** The company's key advantage will give it a significant market share.

Sample Power Paragraph

This power paragraph is for a DepositCash ATM card. (See Chapter 5, page 47 for company description.)

DepositCash ATM Card advantage over pawnshops and other check-cashing businesses is that it allows the direct deposit of paychecks. *[First goal: describe the advantage.]* Direct deposit provides significant savings for employers, and they actively encourage employees to have their paychecks direct-deposited; it also eliminates a 3% to 5% check-cashing fee at traditional check-cashing businesses. *[Second goal: explain why the advantage is important.]* These are two advantages that DepositCash ATM Card's check-cashing competitors don't offer, and they make the DepositCash ATM Card vastly superior for both employers and their employees without banks. *[Third goal: add emphasis appropriate for the business strategy. DepositCash is a market maker; the emphasis for competitive advantage is that the product or service is markedly better than other options.]* DepositCash expects to jump to over 50% market share, following the trend of employers encouraging employees to select the direct-deposit paycheck option. *[Conclusion: the company's key advantage will give it a significant market share.]*

Applicable Plan Sections

1f. Executive Summary—Key Advantage

5. Key Advantage

First Goal: Describe the Advantage

You need to coordinate your key advantage with your market description from Chapter 5. If you've described your market broadly, your advantage has to relate to the broad market. For example, for MediaTile the market was described broadly, as electronic in-store signs. Your advantage should relate to the electronic in-store supermarket sign market, and not just other wireless sign systems. The same applies for a narrow market definition. The Club Runner's market was defined narrowly, as motorized walking carts, and the advantage should relate only to other motorized pull carts, and not to riding carts or traditional walking pull carts.

LOCAL BUSINESSES

Johnson Dental (three dentists and two hygienists serving new housing developments). Johnson Dental will be the first dental office near the target Briarwood and Oakwood developments. The next-closest office is four miles away.

Guitar World (retail store with new and used guitars and accessories). Guitar World's advantage is that it is a gathering spot for budding and current guitarists with 70% of its sales representatives members of bands. It has a performing stage, a wide assortment of equipment, and a band help-wanted bulletin board. These are features not offered by other stores selling equipment.

DISTRIBUTION BUSINESSES

ABC Roofing (supplies roofing materials to 85 roofing companies). ABC Roofing's advantage is not only its 285 roofing styles, but also its Internet catalog site that allows roofers to quickly show potential options to their high-end customers.

Gannet Sales (supplies and service for a complete line of soft-serve frozen yogurt and smoothie equipment). Gannet Sales has eight service people, so it offers quick service for both soft-serve yogurt and smoothie equipment customers. The next-largest competitor has only two service people covering the same area and that company handles only soft-serve yogurt equipment.

SERVICE BUSINESSES

City Course Catering (exclusive rights to staging events, primarily weddings and rehearsal dinners, in two 1920s-era golf course clubhouses). City Course Catering's advantage is its exclusive contract with the two golf course clubhouses. These two stone buildings were built in the 1920s and have a grand scope and ambience matched by few other venues.

Closed Caption Theatre Technology (closed captioning equipment for theaters for a monthly fee). CCTT is the only company in the market offering closed captioning for theaters and it has an exclusive distribution agreement with the only manufacturer offering this equipment.

PRODUCT-BASED BUSINESSES

Club Runner (battery-operated motorized golf pull cart). Club Runner has the widest distribution in the market, twice that of any competitor, being carried at over 100 on-course pro shops and 400 off-course pro shops and available in every catalog and on every major Internet golf shopping site.

MediaTile Smart Signs (signs with wireless connectivity for retail stores, enabling stores to change in-store signs from the office). MediaTile's advantages are that in less than one hour an operator can set the signs from the office and even program the signs to change at designated times throughout the day, and that MediaTile has the most flexibility for choosing font sizes for messages.

INTERNET BUSINESSES

BankIntelligence (current money market rates, national loan rates, and federal fund rates for banks and investment firms). BankIntelligence's advantage is its research network of 28 people throughout the country posting up-to-date information on the site. Competitors only offer weekly or biweekly news updates.

PokerMania.com (site with poker instruction, supplies, accessories and news on upcoming tournaments by state). PokerMania's key advantage to new players is that it has established itself as the industry leader by forming partnerships with 10 regional poker tournament organizers to offer up-to-date tournament dates, registrations, and results for new and experienced poker enthusiasts.

Second Goal: Explain Why the Advantage Is Important

An advantage is important only if it produces a higher market share for the seller of the service or product. The more important the advantage, the higher the market share will be. Try whenever possible to tie the advantage to a key customer need. Take Gannet Sales as an example. It's important to Gannet's customers that the company has eight service people because soft yogurt and smoothie equipment needs service three to four times per year. Without a big service staff, Gannet's customers would be down at least once or twice per year. Since customers want trouble-free operation, the number of service people is an important advantage.

LOCAL BUSINESSES

Johnson Dental. Studies have shown that new residents of an area tend to go to a very visible dental office that is close to their homes.

Guitar World. Customers with big investments in guitars and amplifiers tend to belong to bands. Fostering a "band-like" atmosphere in the store encourages the best customers to frequently visit the store to see what's happening on the local music scene.

DISTRIBUTION BUSINESSES

ABC Roofing. ABC's large inventory and Web site helps roofers meet a key goal, selling higher-margin custom roof products to their customers. Custom roofing materials are a strong marketing tool for roofers against low-cost roofers using standard shingles from Home Depot or other home improvement stores.

Gannet Sales. Since frozen yogurt and smoothie equipment suffers frequent breakdowns, the only way that customers can have trouble-free operation is to have a support firm with a full-service staff for preventive and corrective maintenance.

SERVICE BUSINESSES

City Course Catering. As couples wait longer to get married, they have more disposable income and want to have a memorable wedding in a site with a high-class ambience. City Catering has two of the best 20 sites in the city for an upscale wedding.

Closed Caption Theatre Technology. Theater owners are under pressure to make movies accessible to everyone. They are willing to offer accessibility for all, including the hearing-impaired, if they can do it for a reasonable monthly cost, as offered by CCTT, in order to avoid litigation.

PRODUCT-BASED BUSINESSES

Club Runner. All the motorized walking carts need to have their batteries charged and occasionally replaced and require other service. Supplies, parts, and repair techniques vary by brand and most shops have chosen to carry just one brand because of servicing issues. Having the most outlets provides Club Runner with a sizeable market share lead over competitors.

MediaTile Smart Signs. Consumers constantly modify their supermarket buying behavior based on in-store signs, always looking for the best bargains. With the instant-change capability offered by MediaTile, stores can use bar codes to compare promoted discounts with actual sales and then adjust the discount, change the product discounted, or change the sign message to achieve optimum sales.

INTERNET BUSINESSES

BankIntelligence. The bank information market grows 6% to 10% per year as banks strive to compete in a market where consumers have the ability to compare prices, rates, and fees over the Internet. Instant information is the only way for banks to survive in an Internet world where customers can compare their rates posted on a Web site without ever talking with a banker.

PokerMania.com. Most poker players start out at smaller tournaments with lower entry fees and less competition. PokerMania's partnerships give it instant access to new players as they search for low-cost tournaments on the PokerMania site, the only site where the information for certain tournaments is posted.

Third Goal: Add Emphasis Appropriate for the Business Strategy

Each of the seven business strategies from Chapter 1 requires a slightly different focus regarding competitive advantage.

MARKET MAKER

Key emphasis point: the company's key advantage will give it a significant market share.

MediaTile Smart Signs. Over 50% of supermarket owners in a market research sample preferred MediaTile Smart Signs to any other product in the market because they took less time to program, they coordinated feedback between signs and sales, and offered more visual flexibility.

MARKET ENABLER

Key emphasis point: market advantage is recognized by other players in the market, so that they will promote the company's product or service in order to help market growth.

PokerMania.com. The small regional tournaments appreciate the Web site support and registration features of PokerMania and all of the tournament sponsors tout PokerMania at tournaments and list the PokerMania Web site as a location to check on upcoming tournaments and past tournament winners.

TECHNOLOGY LEADER

Key emphasis point: the new technology will be easy to implement.

Closed Captioning Theatre Technology. CCTT's technology has been field-tested by the manufacturer for over 18 months and has resolved the technical issues of attaching to a seat, removing when not needed, and allowing adjustments so the user can put the captioning in the screen location that he or she prefers. CCTT customers should be able to implement closed captioning without any problems.

NICHE MARKETER

Key emphasis point: people in the market instantly recognize or are moved to buy the product or service because of the competitive advantage.

Guitar World. Guitar World is currently visited by most guitar players in bands at least once per month, and 97% of customer surveys state that Guitar World is the customers' number-one guitar and accessory store.

CUSTOMER SOLUTION

Key emphasis point: the advantage provides customers with a noticeably better solution.

Gannet Sales. Gannet's customers don't want any problems; if they do have one, they want it resolved with a single phone call. Gannet's service staff has a service person in every major city and its staff is on call seven days per week for emergency service. No other company matches that performance.

PERFORMANCE ENHANCER

Key emphasis point: the competitive advantage results in increased sales.

Club Runner. Golf retailers and pro shops, to simplify service, tend to only carry one brand of motorized golf cart. Having the largest distribution network provides the Club Runner top market visibility and the highest potential for increase as the market continues its fast growth.

EFFICIENCY IMPROVER

Key emphasis point: increased efficiency is of substantial value to the customer.

ABC Roofing. ABC's customer base consists of established roofers whose biggest competition comes from new, low-cost roofers that offer standard shingle varieties. ABC's high-value shingles allow its customers to offer a high-value option to homeowners, upscale builders, and architects, a key aspect of ABC's roofing contractor customers' ability to compete.

Conclusion: The Company's Key Advantage Will Give It a Significant Market Share

LOCAL BUSINESSES

Johnson Dental. Johnson Dental's first-to-the-new-market approach will allow it to secure a steady stream of business before any competitors locate in the same area. Since satisfied dental patients rarely change to new dentists unless they move, Johnson Dental should be able to maintain its major market share in upcoming years.

Guitar World. Guitar players trust other guitar players and often buy equipment based on their recommendations. Guitar World's efforts to cater to band members not only bring guitar players to the store, but also allow buyers to get recommendations for their next purchase from both the staff, who are primarily band members, and from other musicians. This extra level of support and encouragement is unmatched in the market and Guitar World expects to gain and maintain a 50% market share.

DISTRIBUTION BUSINESSES

ABC Roofing. ABC Roofing is the largest independent roofing supplier in its area and its broad product line is a major advantage to customers. Most important for future sales, though, is the fact ABC's large inventory can be justified only by a substantial sales level that other distributors don't have. As a result ABC anticipates keeping or growing its market share over the next three years.

Gannet Sales. Currently Gannet has an 80% market share

due to its extensive service network and broad product line and the company expects that market to hold as its competitors have not chosen or are unable to add the level of support the customers need.

SERVICE BUSINESSES

City Course Catering. City Course Catering has increased the number of dates its sites are rented 10% per year for the last three years and has over 85% of available weekend dates filled. City Course Catering is raising its fees 10% and still expects to hold or increase its number of rentals as the market increasingly moves toward upscale event settings.

Closed Caption Theatre Technology. CCTT has the only proven system available in the market. A local advocacy group for the hearing-impaired in Philadelphia reports that 30% of theaters are considering adding closed captioning, so the company expects to capitalize on the growing demand and increase sales 100% per year through 2008.

PRODUCT-BASED BUSINESSES

Club Runner. Motorized walking golf carts follow a typical sales pattern: one or two "pioneers" at a golf club buy a unit, typically for health reasons, and then 10 to 30 others buy after seeing the product on the course. Having the widest distribution, Club Runner sells most of the pioneer units and then the subsequent follow-on units.

MediaTile Smart Signs. In the low-margin competitive supermarket business, results count for every promotion. MediaTile's ability to quickly shift promotions and promotion levels offers customers the chance to optimize their profits. Most MediaTile customers report that the MediaTile system is an investment they should have made earlier than they did.

INTERNET BUSINESSES

BankIntelligence. Banks currently are extremely profitable and they are buying more information than ever before. The benefits of instant information, both to margins and to efforts to capture new customers, are significant and BankIntelligence should be able to continue its rapid sales growth.

PokerMania. 15% of PokerMania's registered users have purchased products and the partnerships with regional tournament sponsors have increased site visits by 300%. PokerMania is negotiating with other tournament sponsors and expects the number of site visitors and their subsequent product purchases to continue to grow.

Chapter 16
Margins: Predicting
Business Strength

Gross and net margins indicate a business's profitability and are key items that investors and bankers evaluate closely. Gross margin typically refers to a profit from sales. It is listed as a percentage, and is calculated by the following formula:

$$\text{gross margin} = \frac{(\text{price} - \text{cost to produce})}{\text{price}} \times 100\%$$

If you have a service business and your hourly price is $90 and your direct costs (including labor, transportation, and supplies) are $45, your margin is 50%.

$$\text{gross margin} = \frac{(\$90 - \$45)}{\$90} \times 100\% = 50\%$$

Net margin typically refers to your total sales dollars. The formula is your total sales, less your cost to produce, less sales, administrative, and other costs (except interest, taxes, and depreciation) divided by the price.

$$\text{net margin} = \frac{(\text{total sales}) - (\text{cost to produce}) - (\text{sales, admin. etc.})}{\text{total sales}} \times 100\%$$

If total sales are $80,000, total cost to produce is $55,000, and total other costs is $17,000, the net margin would be 10%.

$$\text{net margin} = \frac{(\$80{,}000 - \$55{,}000 - \$17{,}000)}{\$80{,}000} \times 100\% = 10\%$$

Margins vary among different types of business. You need to show that your business has margins at least as high as the typical margins for your type of business, if not higher. Your actual margins will be in your financial statements in the plan; if you are not sure where they are, ask whoever prepared the financials for you. Compare those margins with standard industry margins. If you are not sure what the margin for your business should be, contact your local Small Business Development Center, which you can find at www.sba.org, or look in the *Almanac of Business and Industrial Financial Ratios* by Leo Troy (Aspen Publishers, annual), which can be found in the resource section at many larger libraries.

Power Paragraph

Elements of the Power Paragraph

- **First goal:** State what your margins are and how they compare with typical margins.
- **Second goal:** Explain the business factors that allow you to have strong margins.
- **Third goal:** Add emphasis appropriate for the business strategy.
- **Conclusion:** Emphasize that your margins will continue to be strong.

Sample Power Paragraph

This power paragraph is for Embedded Antenna Design, an OEM supplier to manufacturers of wireless applications. The company provides standard and custom antennas for personal digital assistants, computers, remote alarm systems, and utility meter reading.

> Embedded Antenna Design has gross margins of 48% and net margins of 12%, compared with electronic industry norms of 37% and 8%. *[First goal: state what your margins are and how they compare with typical margins.]* Embedded Antenna Design's margins are higher because it offers a high percentage of high-margin custom systems, which allow for a simple interface with the OEM's hardware. *[Second goal: explain the business factors that allow you to have strong margins.]* Embedded Antenna Design custom products eliminate interference and stray signals, simplifying the OEM's design challenge. *[Third goal: add emphasis appropriate for the business strategy. Embedded Antenna Design offers a customer solution, so the emphasis is that a solution is important to customers.]* The company anticipates that its early account penetration and superior design team will allow it to continue to have industry-leading margins well into the future. *[Conclusion: emphasize that your margins will continue to be strong.]*

Applicable Plan Sections

1j. Executive Summary—Sales History/Projections/Margins
8. Company Operations
10. Financial Section

First Goal: State What Your Margins Are and How They Compare with Typical Margins

Your margins will come from the financial balance sheets you do for the plan. If you have never done a balance sheet before, visit your local Small Business Development Center, which you can find at www.sba.gov.

LOCAL BUSINESS

Claire's Discount Perfumes (offers perfume knockoffs, overstocks, and purchases from stores going out of business, all at prices substantially below department store prices). Claire's Discount Perfumes' gross margins average 60% and net margins average 15%, compared with most stores' 45% to 50% gross margins and 3% to 8% net margins.

Design Upgrade Home Lighting (offers high-end lighting features rather than the economy-grade lighting available at home centers and mass merchandiser stores). Design Upgrade Home Lighting's gross margin is 52% and its net margin is 7.3%, typical margins for a mid- to upper-level lighting store.

DISTRIBUTION BUSINESSES

W1 Systems (sells, installs, and supports a wide variety of enterprise distribution and warehouse management software applications for small to mid-size companies, configuring them for each company's operations). W1 Systems maintains a 55% gross margin and a 12% net margin, compared with the industry norms of 40% and 6% to 7%.

All Kitchen Distributors (rack jobber distributor, a wholesaler that purchases space in supermarkets, convenience stores, and large drugstores to sell a wide range of kitchen utensils and then receives its percentage when the utensils sell). All Kitchen Distributors has a 35% gross margin and a 6% net margin, substantially above the typical rack jobber margins of 25% and 4%.

SERVICE BUSINESSES

Peterson's Residential Solution (offers residential service for mentally challenged people living in family, apartment, or group settings). Peterson's Residential Solution's gross margins are 25% and its net margins are 7%, versus an industry average of 20%-22% and 5%.

Holiday Decorations (puts up, takes down, and stores holiday decorations on an annual fee basis for residents, communities, and businesses). Holiday Decorations' gross margins are 40%, and its net margins are 15%, much higher than a typical service business's, with 25% to 35% gross margin and 4% to 8% net margin.

PRODUCT-BASED BUSINESSES

Eyecon Therapeutics (offers products, over the counter or under a private label, to combat dry eye syndrome, a condition endured by approximately 30 to 50 million Americans). Eyecon Therapeutics' gross margin is 60% and its net margin is 15%, about 30% more than typical over-the-counter margins of 45% and 10%.

CottaZilk (produces a new type of fabric, a hybrid of silk and cotton, with the look and feel of silk and the cleaning ease of cotton). CottaZilk market tests indicate that it can be sold for 40% more than silk, which results in gross margins of 28% and net margins of 7%, versus traditional silk gross margins of 15% to 18% and net margins of 4% to 5%.

INTERNET BUSINESS

Tickets-on-Line.com (Web site where people can buy and sell unwanted purchased tickets, with its advantage over eBay being that it guarantees the tickets by taking a credit card slip from the seller to enable refunds in case of fraud). Tickets-on-Line.com's gross margin is over 80% and its net margins are 20%, typical margins for a consignment goods Web site.

Hotcoupons.com (Web site that offers a wide variety of manufacturers' coupons to users and collects a percentage when the coupons are used). Gross margins are over 85% and net margins are 10%. Gross margins are typical of a retailer that offers only paper coupons, while net margins are 50% lower than typical successful Internet sites. The margins will increase as volume increases.

Second Goal: Explain the Business Factors That Allow You to Have Strong Margins

There is probably a substantial reason why your margins are better than other companies achieve or at least equivalent to them. You need to offer a brief explanation here why your margins are higher and why you feel confident that they will remain high.

LOCAL BUSINESS

Claire's Discount Perfumes. Claire is able to maintain the larger margins because the sales mix is tilted heavily towards knockoffs and overstocks, which in some cases have margins of 80%.

Design Upgrade Home Lighting. Designer lighting historically carries high margins and those price levels should be supported in Design Upgrade's upscale mall store and its upscale neighborhood location.

DISTRIBUTION BUSINESSES

W1 Systems. W1 is able to earn these margins due to its software support and its ability to customize each system so it is as easy as possible for the customer to run.

All Kitchen Distributors. All Kitchen's margins are due to offering both economy- and mid-range-priced products side by side, while most jobbers offer only economy products. About 60% of the company's sales are in the higher-margin mid-range products.

SERVICE BUSINESSES

Peterson's Residential Solution. Peterson's margins are

higher since it has focused on group settings where two or more aid workers are needed at once. This focus serves a market that traditionally allows a little higher margin than home businesses. This focus has also cut training and transportation costs.

Holiday Decorations. The company's customer base consists of high-income companies and individuals willing to pay a premium to eliminate the hassle of dealing with their own decorations. Holiday Decorations has avoided the community market, where every job is bid and margins tend to be low.

PRODUCT-BASED BUSINESSES

Eyecon Therapeutics. Current eye drops are designed for temporary eye irritation and not for the persistent problem of dry eye syndrome. The lack of significant competition allows the company to command a premium price for its product.

CottaZilk. Consumers value CottaZilk because it has the elegant look of silk, but is easy to care for. Upscale consumers who don't have time to hand-wash silk much prefer the convenience of CottaZilk.

INTERNET BUSINESS

Tickets-on-Line.com. Tickets-on-Line.com margins depend on keeping the volume high enough to cover the required expenses. Ticket buyers have more confidence with Tickets-on-Line.com's money back guarantee and sales should continue to rise 10% to 15% per quarter, maintaining the company's margins.

Hotcoupons.com. The company needs to increase coupon redemption 50% to raise its margin over 15%. The site attracts 15 or more visits from over 50% of users, and the company expects strong increases in coupon redemption as the site becomes better known.

Third Goal: Add Emphasis Appropriate for the Business Strategy

Each of the seven business strategies from Chapter 1 requires a different comment on why the company can maintain a high margin. A technology leader should address the reader's worry that technology will be difficult to introduce by stating that the technology can be introduced without any major problems, while a performance enhancer should emphasize that the new feature is highly desired by the market, a desire that allows the premium prices that produce high margins.

MARKET MAKER

Key emphasis point: the market wants the product or service and is willing to pay a premium price.

Holiday Decorations. In its first two years of operations, Holiday Decorations has had to limit the number of new clients in order not to be overextended. People don't complain about the pricing; they complain about not being able to get the service.

MARKET ENABLER

Key emphasis point: the market needs the service to grow.

W1 Systems. Without the customization and support, most small- to mid-size firms would not be able to implement this new tier of software. Software suppliers offer special incentives to W1 and customers are willing to pay a fair price for a warehouse and inventory management system that allows them to better serve their customers.

TECHNOLOGY LEADER

Key emphasis point: there are no major production hurdles to introducing the product.

CottaZilk. The company's new technology calls for only minor changes to its traditional silk production methods. The company doesn't expect any major cost changes other than a slightly lower production rate.

NICHE MARKETER

Key emphasis point: the market niche is responsible for the better margins.

Peterson's Residential Solution. Group settings typically pay better than homes, due to the paperwork requirements. Most small suppliers, which make up to 80% of suppliers, shy away from the group homes, as they find the paperwork a burden.

CUSTOMER SOLUTION

Key emphasis point: the complete solution offers a significant benefit to customers.

All Kitchen Distributors. Rack jobbers typically provide a trouble-free solution for the inventory problems due to the small items carried by convenience and drug stores. All Kitchen's solution goes further: its economy- and mid-range-priced stock has increased sales and it helps convenience stores differentiate themselves from the competition.

PERFORMANCE ENHANCER

Key emphasis point: the increased performance provides a significant benefit to the customer.

Tickets-on-Line.com. eBay and other online services don't offer a money-back guarantee, and the real possibility of fraud scares away many potential buyers. This has left most ticket sales to ticket brokers that physically handle the ticket and take a 50% margin. Tickets-on-Line.com costs sellers only a 10% commission, offering them a better price for the tickets while still offering buyers what they want: a money-back guarantee.

EFFICIENCY IMPROVER

Key emphasis point: efficiency results in higher profits.

Claire's Discount Perfumes. Claire's has been able to negotiate lower prices because its volume allows it to take all of an overstock or closed store's inventory, which in turn results in Claire's perfume margins being higher for any store category except department stores.

Conclusion: Emphasize That Your Margins Will Continue to Be Strong

Strong short-term margins are certainly an asset, but you want to be sure that your margins will continue to be strong in the future.

LOCAL BUSINESS

Claire's Discount Perfumes. Claire's owner is a former perfume distributor and she hears first of buying opportunities from her network of distributor contacts. Claire's contacts will enable the store to maintain its margins for the foreseeable future.

Design Upgrade Home Lighting. The Twin Cities West Metro high-end floor, furniture, and home accessory stores have maintained high margins for the last five years and Design Upgrade should be able to maintain the same type of margin performance.

DISTRIBUTION BUSINESSES

W1 Systems. W1 expects competition will enter the market, but that should not affect margins for several years, as most small- to mid-size manufacturers are expected to add warehousing and inventory management software in the next five years in order to meet their customers demands for instant electronic data exchange of shipping information.

All Kitchen Distributors. All Kitchen expects its sales mix of 60% mid-range products to continue as consumers feel the mid-range products are worth twice the money of the economy products, while costing only 33% more.

SERVICE BUSINESSES

Peterson's Residential Solution. Peterson's has a software system in place to simplify the paperwork process and expects its margins to continue to be higher than industry norms as the number of group homes is growing faster than the number of large service providers.

Holiday Decorations. Holiday Decorations is raising money to expand operations to minimize easy entry opportunities for competitors so that it can continue to generate high margins over the next three years.

PRODUCT-BASED BUSINESSES

Eyecon Therapeutics. Eyecon has been in clinical trials for three years to receive FDA approval for an over-the-counter remedy. No trials have been started by potential competitors, so the company expects strong margins for at least five years.

CottaZilk. The company expects margins to remain high with the company's firm production costs and consumers' high-value perception of CottaZilk products.

INTERNET BUSINESS

Tickets-on-Line.com. The company expects increased traffic as the site becomes known as a safe and less costly place to buy and sell unwanted tickets. Tickets-on-Line has closely watched its costs to maintain margins and is confident it can increase its sales faster than its costs to generate even higher margins.

Hotcoupons.com. Hotcoupons.com's new equipment purchases will allow it to increase business 1000%, and it will maintain its current margins with just a 25% increase in coupon redemption. Net margins will increase 1% to 2% with each additional 50% increase in coupon redemptions.

Chapter 17
Start-Up Costs: Justified by the Market Opportunity

Although companies should write business plans regularly, most plans are written to raise money. When evaluating a business plan, bankers and investors ask two major questions: "Is the money enough?" and "Is the money justified by the market size?"

To be successful, a business needs to spend enough money to make an impact in the market. Just as an example, restaurants started with very little money rarely make it in a metropolitan area; they just don't have the ambience to attract customers. Restaurants need to spend enough money to attract customers the first time, and then spend enough money to deliver a quality experience to keep them coming back. Be sure the amount of money requested appears to be enough to impact the market and produce significant sales and profit results.

The second issue is that the amount of money you invest is relevant to the size of the market opportunity. Most investors require that your profits pay back the investment in two to three years. So if you are going to spend $400,000 on a restaurant and your profit margin is 10%, you need to be in an area where the restaurant can produce $2 to $2.5 million per year in sales.

Power Paragraph

- **First goal:** State the amount of money needed and how it will be used.
- **Second goal:** Explain the impact of the investment.
- **Third goal:** If more money will be needed later, explain when and how much.
- **Conclusion:** The money will provide you a significant position in the market.

Sample Power Paragraph

This power paragraph is for Timbuktoo Toys, a toy store featuring unusual foreign toys, with two small stores in upscale neighborhoods, that needs to raise $80,000 to run three mall kiosks in November and December, to generate sales and income and also to promote its two neighborhood stores to new potential customers.

Timbuktoo Toys needs $80,000 for rent deposits, signage, and inventory for three mall kiosks for the months of November and December. *[First goal: state the amount of money needed and how it will be used.]* Based on mall surveys, each kiosk should generate $120,000 or 60% margin sales over the two months. Additionally, mall exposure to potential customers should increase year-round sales at the local stores $50,000 to $75,000. *[Second goal: explain the impact of the investment.]* If the program is successful, the company plans on raising an additional $200,000 to open one mall store. *[Third goal: if more money will be needed later, explain when and how much.]* Timbuktoo Toys' two current successful boutique stores are known only to its loyal customers. The holiday kiosks and subsequent mall opening will position it to be a strong player in the metro high-end toy market. *[Conclusion: the money will provide you a significant position in the market.]*

Applicable Plan Sections

1k. Executive Summary—Start-up costs

4d. Product, Service, or Concept—Explanation of the Proposed Investment

10. Financial Section

First Goal: State the Amount of Money Needed and How It Will Be Used

Don't be overly specific in your power paragraph; just state an overall general purpose. For example, Lopez Dental simply states it needs $175,000 to become an equipment dealer as well as a service agency. This perfect phrase is the most important one in a plan; you need money to do something, so make the phrase easy to remember.

LOCAL BUSINESSES
Cuppa Chioda (coffeehouse with emphasis on after-dinner coffees and lattes with desserts and an entertainment area, catering to teens and young adults). Cuppa Chioda needs to invest $280,000 to acquire and remodel the recently vacated storefront next to its store, to upgrade equipment to handle larger crowds, and to upgrade its entertainment area and equipment.

Angie's Day Spa and Wellness Center (day spa in a small mall in an upscale Memphis, Tennessee, neighborhood). Angie's requires a $750,000 investment to open a day spa in a recently vacated furniture store in a small strip mall next to a highly successful kitchen store and Curves women's exercise club.

DISTRIBUTION BUSINESSES
Lopez Dental Dealer (dental service dealership serving primarily Hispanic dentists). Lopez requires $350,000 to expand its operations from a dental service dealer into a full-service equipment dealer, offering equipment, supplies, and service to primarily Hispanic dentists in Southern California.

Galaxy Plastics (distributor of plastic injection molding machines). Galaxy Plastics needs $200,000 to expand its services to include buying and selling used equipment.

SERVICE BUSINESSES

Data Retrieval Service (provides 24 hour data retrieval service, both on disks and hard copy for small businesses and brokerages). Data Retrieval needs $125,000 to build a secure, fireproof room within its warehouse to store sensitive electronic records for small brokers.

Sakodowskis Marketing (retention marketing service through Web-based programs). Sakodowskis requires $350,000 to add the programmers, equipment, and sales support staff to offer its retention services to companies with marketing budgets over $1 million.

PRODUCT-BASED BUSINESSES

Multi-Format Ceramic Tile (offers ceramic tile in a variety of sizes and looks, such as granite or marble). Multi-Format needs to invest $3,250,000 to upgrade to the newest state-of-the-art equipment to maintain its leadership position in the designer ceramic market.

Freeze Frame Cosmetics (cosmetic cream designed to keep the wrinkles out, with the marketing slogan, "Nature not Needles"). Freeze Frame is seeking a $6 million investment to launch a nationwide promotional program.

INTERNET BUSINESSES

Livetutorial.com (Web site matches tutors and students, geared more at non-students who want to learn a skill like woodworking, learn to speak a foreign language, or learn more skills about a hobby). The company is raising $4 million to set up its tutor/student network, to promote its site, and to purchase equipment to conduct uninterrupted tutor sessions.

HomeSaleValues.com (Web site that provides information about recent home sales in any community, including dimensions and features of each home). HomeSaleValues is raising $400,000 to expand from its Texas base to 45 metro areas throughout the country.

Second Goal: Explain the Impact of the Investment

To be worthwhile, an investment has to produce an impact on sales. For example, in the case of Lopez Dental Dealer, the owner wants to expand from service alone to become an equipment dealer so that he can become the sole source of dental equipment and service for his customers. If Lopez provides only service, dentists must buy equipment from other dealers and then get warranty service from the selling dealer. Lopez might be able to invest $150,000 to acquire low-market-share lines, but might need $350,000 to acquire the top dental product lines. The $350,000 investment probably is the best choice; it makes the most impact toward being a sole source supplier.

LOCAL BUSINESSES

Cuppa Chioda. The expansion will triple capacity from 50 to 150 people, allow the coffeehouse to add seven to 10 new menu and drink choices, and allow it to bring in better entertainment on its busy Friday and Saturday nights.

Angie's Day Spa and Wellness Center. This investment will allow Angie's to create a day spa comparable in size, equipment, and amenities to two successful spas that are located in upscale neighborhoods on the other side of Memphis.

DISTRIBUTION BUSINESSES

Lopez Dental Dealer. Becoming a full-service dealer will allow Lopez to be a 100% supplier to its approximately 120 dentist customers. Currently Lopez is an out-of-warranty service supplier, picking up only 10% of its customers' total dental dealer-related business.

Galaxy Plastics. The addition of used equipment will allow Galaxy to offer services similar to those offered by Plastic Molding Equipment, its largest competitor, which has gained a huge edge in the market by being able to take trade-ins when customers upgrade their production equipment.

SERVICE BUSINESSES

Data Retrieval Service. New legislation requires all brokerage houses to have secure backup data with 24-hour retrieval. Data Retrieval needs to add a fireproof, secure room with redundant security backups or lose its customers to other storage services.

Sakodowskis Marketing. Sakodowskis' two principals had extensive retention marketing experience at Risdahl Advertising; this investment will provide the equipment and depth of programming expertise to land the larger, highly profitable accounts.

PRODUCT-BASED BUSINESSES

Multi-Format Ceramic Tile. Two small competitors with new equipment that offer an upscale designer look and more flexibility in tile thickness have posed a threat to Multi-Format's market share. Responding quickly will keep Multi-Format's share intact.

Freeze Frame Cosmetics. Freeze Frame has successfully launched its product in South Florida. The company wants to advertise the product and its success in national magazines to establish the Freeze Frame name before copycat products enter the market.

INTERNET BUSINESSES

Livetutorial.com. Adults, particularly senior citizens, are pursuing hobbies and avocations as never before. Livetutorial offers people access to instructions in any field, especially fields without enough interest for a local class. The site also offers people to share their interest with others through one-to-one instruction.

HomeSaleValues.com. HomeSaleValues.com offers people in-depth information about homes recently sold in the area where they are looking to buy. The site has been popular; with a national base, the company will be able to attract national advertisers and national name recognition.

Third Goal: If More Money Will Be Needed Later, Explain When and How Much

Many businesses practice a staged growth. For example, a cutting tool distributor's first stage of growth might be to serve the small- to medium-size machine shops, with a second expansion to serve large machine shops and machine shops located within large manufacturing facilities. Investors like to see future expansion plans, as expansion offers more opportunities for their shares to increase in value.

LOCAL BUSINESSES

Cuppa Chioda. Cuppa Chioda plans on expanding to new locations, with a location expected to require a $250,000 investment, once it has established a successful model at its initial location.

Angie's Day Spa and Wellness Center. Angie's may expand later, but doesn't have any immediate expansion plans.

DISTRIBUTION BUSINESSES

Lopez Dental Dealer. [Lopez has no further expansion plans, so this goal can be left out of the power paragraph.]

Galaxy Plastics. Galaxy's next expansion plan is to purchase in two years Landmark Plastics, a small distributor with exclusive rights to several lines of rotational molding equipment. That acquisition will give Galaxy the broadest line in the market.

SERVICE BUSINESSES

Data Retrieval Service. The company plans to self fund any future projects so nothing needs to be mentioned in the plan.

Sakodowskis Marketing. Sakodowskis plans on raising money to launch its service into the New York, Boston, and New England markets once its Philadelphia service is established.

PRODUCT-BASED BUSINESSES
Multi-Format Ceramic Tile. This investment will allow Multi-Format to hold market share and, in the future, to self-finance or lease through suppliers the equipment required to match market growth.

Freeze Frame Cosmetics. Freeze Frame plans to capitalize on its brand name by raising $3 to $5 million to expand its product line in 2007.

INTERNET BUSINESSES
Livetutorial.com. Livetutorial.com's initial market effort includes some programmed instructions with paid instructors, but consists mostly of unpaid instructors who are just anxious to help some learn about their avocation. In two years the company expects to raise an additional $10 to $15 million to add a more complete offering of programmed classes.

HomeSaleValues.com. [No additional investments are projected, so this section can be omitted from the plan.]

Conclusion: The Money Will Provide You a Significant Position in the Market

Companies with a market presence can succeed. The conclusion simply states that your investment allows your business to have a significant impact in the market and that people will know who you are.

LOCAL BUSINESSES

Cuppa Chioda. Cuppa Chioda has carefully selected its location in an area with a large local high school population and few other entertainment options for high school students. The planned expansion offers enough seating for Cuppa Chioda to be a preferred night and weekend hangout for the local neighborhood teenagers and young adults.

Angie's Day Spa and Wellness Center. Angie's $750,000 investment will allow it to create the full-service spa favored by upper-class women and allow it to be the dominant spa in its chosen Memphis neighborhood.

DISTRIBUTION BUSINESSES

Lopez Dental Dealer. By expanding to full service, Lopez will become a primary supplier to all of its current customers and Lopez feels it will become a sole source supplier to about 33% of its customer base.

Galaxy Plastics. Adding used equipment will allow Galaxy products to sell to new manufacturers, which are often underfinanced, and establish a relationship with them before they grow into major producers. Currently competitors have this first-supplier position and Galaxy has been forced to use price discounting to get in the door. Adding used equipment will allow Galaxy to compete across the entire market and compete effectively for sales to new plastics manufacturers.

SERVICE BUSINESSES
Data Retrieval Service. The addition of the required storage area for brokerages will allow the company to keep its current customers and also to compete effectively for brokerage business that may open up if competitors fail to respond to the new regulations.

Sakodowskis Marketing. Sakodowskis has a head start as its principals are known in the market. Adding the programming and equipment support will establish the company as market leader in the Philadelphia area.

PRODUCT-BASED BUSINESSES
Multi-Format Ceramic Tile. Multi-Format holds a leading 24% market share; with this investment, the company will continue to offer the state-of-the-art products the market demands.

Freeze Frame Cosmetics. "Nature not Needles" has proven to be a powerful slogan as problems with botox treatments are becoming well known. This major promotional campaign will establish Freeze Frame as the leading natural wrinkle-free cream in the market.

INTERNET BUSINESSES
Livetutorial.com. Livetutorial.com's investment will put it on the leading edge of individualized learning geared to

older adults and will position the company to expand its offerings in the future.

HomeSaleValues.com. By establishing itself first in 46 markets, HomeSaleValues expects to be a popular site for home buyers, which will make it a popular site for companies advertising their real estate services.

Chapter 18
Founder Financing: Show Commitment to the Business

Banks and investors don't want to loan or give you money unless they know that the principals are also heavily invested so they have a lot to lose if the business doesn't succeed. This is especially true if you are just starting out and raising money to begin your business. A term you'll hear from people evaluating business plans is *founding investors*. Founding investors are those who invest when a company is just starting out, which could include family and friends. Banks and investors like to see that start-ups have investments from others; it gives them confidence that other people feel the business has enough merit that they are willing to invest in it. When the business is up and running, banks and investors want to know first that the principals are investing and second that the founding investors, if any, are also investing again. Otherwise, it appears that the founding investors have lost confidence in the business.

Elements of the Power Paragraph

- **First goal:** State the amount of money needed and how much is needed from outside investors or a bank loan.
- **Second goal:** State the company's current funding, which explains how it has been financed to date.
- **Conclusion:** State the company's investments and outstanding loans after this round of financing.

Sample Power Paragraph

This power paragraph is for Timbuktoo Toys, a toy store that needs to raise $80,000 to run three mall kiosks in November and December.

> Timbuktoo Toys needs a total of $80,000 for the three mall kiosks. The company's owner and lead investor can raise $30,000 and the company needs a $50,000 loan. *[First goal: state the amount of money needed and how much is needed from outside investors or a bank loan.]* $160,000 has been invested in Timbuktoo's two current stores—$100,000 from the owner and two investors and a $60,000 bank loan. *[Second goal: state the company's current funding, which explains how it has been financed to date.]* After this round of financing, the company will have $130,000 in investments and $110,000 in bank loans. *[Conclusion: state the company's investments and outstanding loans after this round of financing.]*

Applicable Plan Sections

1I. Executive Summary—Capitalization or Financing Plan

10. Financial Section

First Goal: State the Amount of Money Needed and How Much Is Needed from Outside Investors or a Bank Loan

One of the entrepreneurs' biggest mistakes is that they spend all their money before going out to raise the rest of the money they need. The proper tactic is for an owner to decide on an investment for the company and then hold his or her investment until all the funding is in place. Otherwise, the owner will be borrowing money after he has spent all his money and is essentially broke, which makes the owner appear to be a bad business manager.

LOCAL BUSINESSES

Cuppa Chioda (coffeehouse with emphasis on after-dinner coffees and lattes with desserts and an entertainment area catering to teens and young adults). Cuppa Chioda needs $280,000 for its expansion: $40,000 from the store's founders, $120,000 from additional investors, and $120,000 from a bank loan.

Angie's Day Spa and Wellness Center (day spa in a small mall in an upscale Memphis, Tennessee, neighborhood). $150,000 to open Angie's will come from the founding three family investors. The company is seeking a $600,000 bank loan to complete the financing package.

DISTRIBUTION BUSINESSES

Lopez Dental Dealer (dental service dealership serving primarily Hispanic dentists). Lopez and his family are providing $50,000 and Lopez is seeking a bank loan of $300,000 to cover the rest of the required investment.

Galaxy Plastics (distributor of plastic injection molding machines). Galaxy Plastics is seeking a $200,000 bank loan to initiate its used machinery program.

SERVICE BUSINESSES

Data Retrieval Service (provides 24-hour data retrieval service, both on disks and hard copy for small businesses and brokerages). Data Retrieval is seeking a $75,000 bank loan, to supplement its $50,000 investment for a fireproof, secure data storage room.

Sakodowskis Marketing (retention marketing service through Web-based programs). Sakodowskis' founders can fund $80,000 of the $350,000 investment themselves and are applying for a bank loan for $270,000.

PRODUCT-BASED BUSINESSES

Multi-Format Ceramic Tile (offers ceramic tile in a variety of sizes and looks, such as granite or marble). The company is having a private round of financing through the investment banking firm of Miller and Smith to raise the $3.25 million needed.

Freeze Frame Cosmetics (cosmetic cream designed to keep the wrinkles out with the marketing slogan, "Nature not Needles"). Freeze Frame has signed a joint private agreement/investment agreement with Premier Cosmetics (for the hair salon market) and is seeking the remaining $3 million from no more than five private investors.

INTERNET BUSINESSES

Livetutorial.com (Web site matches tutors and students, geared more at non-students who want to learn a skill like woodworking, learn to speak a foreign language, or learn more skills about a hobby). Livetutorial.com's founders and founding investors are contributing $1 million of the $4 million investment, with the remaining money being raised with a private stock offering through Brainbridge and Johnson.

HomeSaleValues.com (Web site that provides information about recent home sales in any community, including dimensions and features of each home). The company founders are investing $50,000 of the $400,000, two mortgage companies are each investing $75,000 in return for preferred advertising placements, and the company is seeking a bank loan for the remaining $200,000.

Second Goal: State the Company's Current Funding, Which Explains How It Has Been Financed to Date

How much has been invested in the company prior to this round of financing is critical. Someone looking to loan money wants to know what other loan obligations exist, as that effects the company's ability to pay off this new loan. An investor wants to know how many shares are outstanding, so he or she understands how much of the business his or her investment will buy. If you are selling stock and the founder or current principals have made a large investment, you can also state how much of the stock is owned by the founder or current principals.

LOCAL BUSINESSES

Cuppa Chioda. Cuppa Chioda's $85,000 investment to date has been entirely funded by the owners.

Angie's Day Spa and Wellness Center. Prior to this point, Angie's founders have funded approximately $20,000 in legal, accounting, and market research expenses themselves.

DISTRIBUTION BUSINESSES

Lopez Dental Dealer. Lopez started the business with an $18,000 investment and a $15,000 bank loan. The loan has been repaid and, over the last seven years, $42,000 in profits has been reinvested in the company's operations.

Galaxy Plastics. Galaxy Plastics was started with a $25,000 line of credit from a major supplier and the owner's willingness to work six months without a salary. The business currently has a $75,000 line of credit from its major manufacturers that covers consignment inventory and allows Galaxy, on major orders, to wait to pay the manufacturers until Galaxy's customers pay. Galaxy has invested $30,000 in profits into a business showroom, computer equipment, and a spare parts inventory.

SERVICE BUSINESSES

Data Retrieval Service. The company's principals and founding investors have invested $60,000 in the company and the company has a $62,000 balance on an original $85,000 loan.

Sakodowskis Marketing. The Sakodowskis have invested $12,000 from their savings to date for business start-up costs.

PRODUCT-BASED BUSINESSES

Multi-Format Ceramic Tile. The company up to this time has issued 2.6 million shares of stock with an average price of $1.28 per share, for a capitalization of $3.28 million. This round of financing will sell 1 million shares of stock for $3.25 per share.

Freeze Frame Cosmetics. Freeze Frame has invested $2.6 million in product development and initial product marketing in Florida. 6.75 million shares of stock are outstanding, with 4 million held by the founder, with an average acquisition cost of $0.38.5 per share. The company is selling 3 million shares at $2 per share in this round of financing.

INTERNET BUSINESSES

Livetutorial.com. The company founders and original investors have given the company to date $250,000 in funding and own 2.5 million shares of stock. The company is selling 4 million shares, 1 million of which are being acquired by the founder and founding investors, at $1 per share.

HomeSaleValues.com. HomeSaleValues.com's founders have invested $20,000 in business start fees, including legal fees.

Conclusion: State the Company's Investments and Outstanding Loans After This Round of Financing

For companies borrowing money, the key is what percentage of the company's total investment is in loans. With a stock sale, the bigger concern is what percent of the company the founder and founding investors will have and what percent of the company the new investors will own.

LOCAL BUSINESSES

Cuppa Chioda. After this investment, the company's founders' investment will be $125,000, for which they will own 70% of the company's stock, outside investors will have invested $125,000 and will own 30% of the stock, and the company will carry a $120,000 bank loan.

Angie's Day Spa and Wellness Center. Once the spa opens, the owner and family investors will have put $170,000 into the business to go along with a $600,000 bank loan.

DISTRIBUTION BUSINESSES

Lopez Dental Dealer. After the bank loan, Lopez and his family investors will have put $110,000 into the company and will have borrowed $300,000.

Galaxy Plastics. Once funding is secured, the company will have a $30,000 total investment from Galaxy's owners, a $75,000 credit line from its suppliers that is directly related to orders received, and a $200,000 bank loan.

SERVICE BUSINESSES

Data Retrieval Service. Once the new $75,000 loan is secure, Data Retrieval's owners will have invested $110,000 and be carrying a loan debt of $137,000.

Sakodowskis Marketing. Upon funding, $96,000 of the start-up funds will come from the company principals and $270,000 from a bank loan.

PRODUCT-BASED BUSINESSES

Multi-Format Ceramic Tile. If financing is successful, the company will have 3.6 million shares and a total capitalization of $11.7 million. The company founder and founding investors will own 2.1 million or 58% of the shares and new investors will own 27.7% of the company.

Freeze Frame Cosmetics. Upon sale of the 3 million shares, the company will have 9.75 million shares outstanding at a total value of $19.5 million. The founder will hold 41% of the shares and new investors will control 30.7% of the company stock.

INTERNET BUSINESSES

Livetutorial.com. The company founder and founding investors, after fundraising is complete, will own 3.5 million shares and new investors will own 3 million shares. The company's capitalization value will be $6.5 million.

HomeSaleValues.com. The company founder owns 70% of the stock and the total invested in the company, including from the founder and partnership companies, is $220,000, slightly more than the $200,000 loan that the company is seeking.

PERFECT PHRASES
for...

MANAGERS

Perfect Phrases for
Managers and Supervisors

Perfect Phrases for Setting
Performance Goals

Perfect Phrases for
Performance Reviews

Perfect Phrases for
Motivating and Rewarding
Employees

Perfect Phrases for
Documenting Employee
Performance Problems

Perfect Phrases for Business
Proposals and Business Plans

Perfect Phrases for
Customer Service

Perfect Phrases for
Executive Presentations

Perfect Phrases for Business
Letters

Perfect Phrases for the
Sales Call

Perfect Phrases for Perfect
Hiring

Perfect Phrases for Building
Strong Teams

Perfect Phrases for Dealing
with Difficult People

YOUR CAREER

Perfect Phrases for the
Perfect Interview

Perfect Phrases for
Resumes

Perfect Phrases for Negotiating
Salary & Job Offers

Perfect Phrases for Cover
Letters

Learn more. Do more.

Visit mhprofessional.com/perfectphrases for a complete product listing.